Mo2's
Financial Freedom
Wisdom

M. "Mo2" Shimizu

Mo2's Financial Freedom Wisdom

Website:

Mo2thinks.com

Cover Artist Information:

Artist: Moochirin
Website:
Moochirin.devianart.com

Table of Contents

Section 3: Everyday Life Tidbits
How one less Vanilla Latte a week can save you $20,000
Smoking Less could you more than your Life
Save on Banking and Credit Card Fees
Save First and Buy Later or Never
Understanding Your Current Lifestyle

Section 4: Dealing with Debt
Don't Cut up Your Credit Card!
Smart Debt vs. Stupid Debt
Paying Down Your Mortgage Faster
The Best Guaranteed Investment with no Risk, Get out of Debt!

Section 5: Tying it All Together
Discipline
Be Generous when it counts
Understand who you are and what your life goals are
Keep it Simple!
The Lifelong Goal of Financial Freedom
Closing Notes

Introduction

I love reading and studying about personal finance and investing. Anytime I have the chance, I'm reading up a new website/blog, article or book about these two topics. Yes according to a good friend of mine, I know nothings other than financial planning and investments. Playing the guitar apparently doesn't count as knowledge. Who knew?

My goal with this book is to help people become a little more financially savvy. I live in Canada where we are considered to be the most educated country in the world. Look it up, you might be surprised.

That's impressive and there's no wonder why Canada's job market is so competitive. But that's beside my point. As a banker that has met tens of thousands of clients, I can tell you that while our population may be educated, they sure aren't financially educated.

We aren't as bad as our counterparts down south, but our savings to debt ratio has continued to fall and many people are so much debt they really don't understand how much trouble they are in. So if Canada is like this, you can only imagine what the rest of the world is like. Having said all that, there are countries out there that save much more than people in North America.

Most people focus on how to earn more money and rarely think about the other end of the spectrum. That is, what they are spending their money on. They only think about the needs and mostly wants (think Hermes bags, extravagant vacations, expensive restaurants, and the like) and don't think about the tax advantages they should taking advantage of or how to save a little money here and there and more importantly what they should be doing with the money they save.

When was the last time that you actually sat down and looked at all of the money you made and looked at every single penny that you spent in the past month, quarter, or even year? If you have, then you're well on your way and you most likely don't need to read this book. But if you haven't, do you realize how important that little hassle is?

I'm not telling you to be cheap, I'm only remotely telling you to be frugal. You don't have to cut corners or live like you're earning pennies, (although it feels like we are doesn't it?) I'm asking you to be conscious of how you spend your money and how big of a difference it makes by simply being conscious of how you spend your money.

I'll throw a random number at you just to give you some context. If you were to save a mere $25 a week over the next 30 years and put that away in a mutual fund with an average return of 6%, in 30 years you'll have $109,273.09. Yes you read that right and yes I have checked my math. If you save $25 and put that money away every week at 6%, you'll have over a hundred grand. Should I repeat that?

This is why it's so important for you to be conscious of how you spend your money. Multiply that by 4-6 times and it'll take care of most people's retirement fund. You think I'm joking right? Well let's look at another number.

Unless you live in Vancouver, like I do where the cost of living doesn't go up in percentage points but exponentially, you don't need crazy amounts to retire. The average person only needs $2,000-$2,500 a month after tax to live very comfortably. Obviously, it all depends on where you live in the world and this number may be much lower (likely) or higher in some parts of the world.

At $2,000 a month you need $24,000 a year. If we take tax into consideration and your average tax rate is 25%, then you need $32,000 per year. You might think 25% is low, and if it is, then recalculate that number with the actual tax rate you would be paying. (Calculated as $24,000/(1-x%)). Ok before you close the book I'm talking math and you hate math. Trust me, this one calculation is worth it. I know you're probably thinking, "I'll come back to this later." No, not happening. Go get a calculator this minute and punch in your number. This is very important! No procrastinating is permitted with this book!

At the 6% return we used earlier, you'll need $533,333 invested in order to get $32,000 a year. Now that's if you are getting distributions or returns for the 6% at your highest taxable income. Some countries, like Canada, have different forms of income like dividend tax credits and capital gains where you are taxed differently for the type of income you earn. So in fact if you can create an investment portfolio to give you distributions that give you a tax advantage, then the actual amount you will need will be much lower than $533,333, probably closer to $400,000-$450,000. And well, you should check your local government's tax brackets, because it might actually be lower than 25%.

To use Canada as an example, at the time of writing this book, specifically in Vancouver since each province pays different taxes, we pay around 20.06% for the first $37,013. At 20.06%, we actually only need around $30,000 income per year. We also don't have to pay taxes on roughly the first $10,000 so in fact you really only need to pay taxes on $20,000 ($30,000-$10,000=$20,000) of your annual income. This means that at 20.06% you only need to have an investment portfolio of $333,333, which is much lower than the initial $533,333. And again this is without having tax efficient returns and distributions, which mean you, have the potential to reduce this number even more.

So now all of a sudden these numbers seem much more achievable. Now to get back to the weekly calculation. If we said we needed $300,000 in 30 years (taking into consideration, some tax efficient distributions), then you actually only need to save $68.64 per week.

That was a mouthful of an introduction, but I hope I was able to open your eyes. $68.64 is not a big number. Even if you don't have 30 years or can't see yourself making 6% (which is actually very possible), then you may need to increase that number but even then, if you take the time to plan things out, stick to the plan, and be conscious of your spending, you're actually a lot closer to financial freedom than you might think.

This is the foundation about what this book is about. I want you to understand the importance of how small things can add to huge results. I'll talk about how you can save the $68 a week or whatever your number turns out to be, but more importantly I'll talk about what you need to focus on to be conscious about your financial education. I'll also talk about understanding what financial freedom really is what it will help you achieve in life. We get caught up in all the small things in life that we forget to look at things from a bigger perspective.

What's Your Number?

So the first question you need to ask yourself is, "What is that magic number I need in order to achieve financial freedom?" Every single individual will have a different number. This is because we are all in different life stages, have different family situations, different lifestyles, needs, wants and obligations. That's why you can't go with a cookie cutter number and have to spend some time looking at your specific numbers.

The first step is to look at the money you are spending currently. And I mean down to the last penny. So this means you'll need to do some work. Pull out your most recent bank statements. In this day and age, you should easily be able to pull this information up through your online banking platform. Don't know how? Well it's time to learn. As much as it's nice to go to the bank, it's a complete waste of time. I'm a banker and I use the teller maybe 3 times a year, I'm dead serious.

We call this a cash flow analysis to see how you are doing in terms of the money you make and the money you spend.

Punch in the numbers and you should see what your total positive (you have extra cash, yes!) and negative (you're gonna lose your shirt at this rate...) cash flow numbers. You obviously want to come out ahead and being positive is extremely important but we'll get to that in another section. Right now I want you to figure out what your monthly expenses are.

This means we need to know how much you are spending on rent, utilities, transportation, groceries, education, savings, entertainment, dining out, beer, coffee, donations, vacations, and everything else. If there are certain things that you don't do every month, like donations and vacations then think of that in an annual sense and divide that number by twelve.

Let's simplify it and think of what you spend on a monthly basis.

Why Do You Want to Save Money?

If you've picked up any money-saving book or read blogs about budgeting before, you'll see a lot of the same money saving tidbits. My book isn't going to be too different as far as the basic concepts, I'm not trying to reinvent the wheel, I am however, trying to give you a different perspective about saving money. Just as with other aspects of life, you need to look at the big picture to be successful. Saving money is only one slice of the pie, and it all comes down to your purpose behind saving money and what you do with the money saved.

Why do you want to save money? Having a purpose makes a life of a difference. Is it to fund your children's education? In order retire early and retire wealthy? Or is it so that you can have a little more breathing room so that you don't live paycheck to paycheck? Maybe it's a combination of everything. You need to figure out why you want to save money and write it down. Writing your goals down and keeping track and rewarding yourself on the way to your goal is extremely important.

But don't just have vague goals, actually try and figure out what the estimated amount of funds you will need to achieve the goal. For example, if you are saving money to fund your children's post-secondary education figure out how much tuition, monthly living expenses, textbooks, etc. will cost for the amount of time they go to school. If you're saving money for retirement, how much will you actually need on a monthly basis after-tax, to be living happily? By having a ballpark figure, it will help you visualize what you need to do to achieve that goal and with a little calculation, you'll know how much you need to save regularly. Instead of trying to eat the whole pie at once, it's much more manageable and easy to digest if you snack away at it in pieces. Trust me, I've tried eating a whole pie at once, my stomach hated me after this endeavor.

The Importance of Financial Responsibility
By learning to budget and save money, you are improving your financial responsibility. There are countless benefits in becoming financially responsible. You'll be a lot more disciplined when you spend your money on daily purchases and will do you due diligence before making a bigger purchase. As a result of being financially responsible, it will help your credit rating and this helps

you borrow money from the bank, usually at lower interest rates compared to those that aren't financially responsible.

Financial responsibility goes a long way, and you can teach this to your family and friends and eventually your children. It makes everyone around you happy because everyone will have better control over his or her finances. I firmly believe that it isn't how much you earn; it's what you do with the money you earn that makes a difference. This is the mindset that you need to engrave in your mind. If you save and budget properly and invest on a regular basis while having all your bases covered for emergencies, you will be much better off that people that are making double or even triple your income that spend all of their money on useless items.

Don't be Sensitive About Money

Many people are scared to talk about money. If you talk about their spending habits, many people will get defensive and get angry with you. Most people are insecure and know they're not taking care of their finances as best as they should. At the same time most of these people are too proud to try and learn. I've seen many people that earn high wages that can't seem to hold on to their earnings and be happy with life.

Be open to new concepts and devote a part of your life to keep studying to become financially intelligent. You honestly can't lose out, and by doing this you will help people around. Your family and friends will depend on you for financial advice and it will help future generations in your family. You might even be able to create a legacy

13

that stands tall for many generations to come, it certainly is a possibility and it's entirely up to you.

There are a lot of "specialists" and "professionals" around us. You can go to any bank branch and there will always be so-called professionals giving you advice. I've worked for one of the biggest banks in the world and can tell you first hand that most of these "professionals", even with their well known 3 letter designations often don't know what they're talking about. Even if they do know what they're talking about, many of them are thinking about the commissions they can get and giving great advice isn't always in their best interests.

By being financially independent, you won't have to hire these professionals. But if you don't have the time to manage your finances, at least to the extent that you would like, then you will be able to filter out the bad professionals and find highly intelligent individuals that will actual put your interests before theirs. They're hard to find, but there are people out there that genuinely want to help. If you find someone like that, you should do everything to recommend him or her to your friends and family because you've found a gem.

I commend you for taking the time to read this book. It shows that you care about saving money and dealing with your finances. But my hope is that you have bigger goals and dreams in mind. Have a reason for saving this money, keep track of how much you save and reward yourself on your lifetime journey. You'll end up a lot happier if you do these three things.

<u>Why Having a Monthly Budget is So Important</u>

Now that you have spent the time to take an average of your monthly expenses, you need to analyze where you can save more money. Break down your daily expenses and ask yourself if you really needed to spend money on those new shoes or if you really have to have a latte at Starbucks every 6 hours. Believe it or not, setting a monthly budget is one of the most important steps to savings a large amount of money and I think I hit that thought home in the first page or two of this book.

Let's take a look at an example. Here is Mr. Kazuyoshi's monthly budget.

Rent or Mortgage:	$1,000
Groceries:	$ 200
Hydro/Electricity:	$ 50
Phone Bill:	$ 50
Internet Bill:	$ 50
Insurance:	$ 200
Gas:	$ 150
Savings:	$ 150
Dining Out:	$ 250
Clothing:	$ 100
Coffee:	$ 100
Misc.:	$ 300
Total:	<u>$2,600</u>

The point here is to simply illustrate that we have come up with a number that we can compare our actual expenses to on a monthly basis. In reality, your numbers may be higher or lower to this. Don't feel the need to adjust your spending according to this budget because depending on where you live in the world, living expenses will be very different so it really depends on where you are and how much you earn.

So now that you know how much you spend and you've analyzed your spending you now know your monthly expenses. You should now compare this to how much you earn after-tax. If you earn $3,000 after-tax and you have the above budget of $2,600 you're doing alright because you have an excess of $400. But if you earn $2,000 you're obviously going over budget and need to cut costs somewhere.

If you are indeed spending more than your monthly after-tax income, you need to look closer at what you are spending money on. Are you dining out too much? Could you be packing lunch more often? Do you really need to buy all that coffee? Can't you bring your own coffee/tea to work? What constitutes the miscellaneous spending?

This step is extremely important because you need to sort out the necessities and the luxuries. Yes, a latte is a luxury if you don't "need" it. Remember, every penny saved is a penny that goes towards your goals.

Say, you've decided that you can actually cut down your coffee spending to $50 a month and your Misc. to $200. Now you've lowered your monthly budget by $150 and are down to $2,450. Great job! This is now officially your monthly budget.

So the next month you are now conscious of your spending. When the end of the month rolls around you realize you actually met your goals and spent $2,400 compared to the $2,450 that you budgeted for! Extremely good job, so your next job is to reward yourself! You have a number of ways to reward yourself but I suggest you implement the 50/50 rule.

The 50/50 rule is where you use the excess amount of money to use half of the money saved for yourself and the other half on savings or investing. So that means you can spend $25 of the $50 you saved on a decent dinner or movie date and the other $25 on saving for that new computer you've been wanting to get! Doesn't it feel great to reward yourself for saving money and beating your monthly budget? I'll talk more about the 50/50 rule in a later chapter.

So say a few months pass and you've been given the wonderful news that you're getting a raise at work! You find out that your monthly pay will actually increase by $400 per month after-tax! That's a very nice increase and it means you can spend more right? Wrong! Now that you are used to your monthly budget you stay exactly where you are and continue to spend according to the monthly budget you already have laid out. This way you will be able to save more money for your goals and dreams and because of the extra income you are now getting, you will be able to achieve those goals that much quicker! But of course you can still implement the 50/50 rule so whatever extra you have at the end of the month you're allowed to do anything you want with.

Sure it'll be very tempting for you to spend a little more money here and there but this is where you need to have strong will power. If you must, you can increase some parts of your budget such as dining out but you have to ensure that a significant portion of your pay increase is going straight to your savings or paying down any debt that you have outstanding.

Remember to review your monthly budget on a regular basis! As you become even more financially intelligent, you might find ways to save more money. There might be a cheaper and better insurance policy out there for you if you do a little shopping. You might find great tips right here in this book to save you more money, don't be shy! Implement those tips right away, every dollar saved puts you a dollar closer to achieving your goals.

How a Small Side Income can make a Huge Difference in the Long Term

So let's do a little calculation. Remember the $25 a week that we talked about at the beginning of the book, and how that $25 could turn into over $100,000 in 30 years? That's what this small side income to do to you. If you could earn an extra $200 a month it could literally make a life of a difference.

In the previous chapter you worked on setting your budget and your regular income should easily be covering your monthly expenses. By earning this extra income you will be putting a huge dent into any outstanding debt or will be increasing your savings significantly at a much faster pace than just relying on your employment income.

Here are some sources of side income that you could consider:
Regular Basis:
Any Part-time Job

Selling Used Books
Sell all Unused and Unwanted Items at Home on eBay or Craigslist
Freelance on sites like elance.com
Write a Blog and Monetize it
Become a Real Estate Investor – Income from Tenants
Invest in Dividend Paying Stocks
Affiliate Marketing (ie have referral links on your website that lead people to buy on places like Amazon)
Garage Sale (you obviously can't do this every month)
Bake Sale

That's just a small list of infinite possibilities. Use your creativity to find ways of making some extra cash. It's always nice to do something you enjoy especially if you are going to be spending time outside of your work schedule. If you work full time, an extra part-time job can be really draining so try and find something that'll benefit you or you find some interest in.

Of course, you could always ask for a pay raise too if you feel you deserve it, although your manager might not always agree. You can always look for another job in the same line of work, an easy way to get a raise is to change companies. Of course, take this advice with a grain of salt. You're probably comfortable with your current employment situation. You might like your colleagues or you might have a great company or manager, these factors are often more important than money.

Once you figure out how you're going to earn some extra cash, plan out how you're going to save it. We'll talk about investing in more detail later on in this book. You also want to reward yourself for spending time for the extra income. You can implement the 50/50 rule again by saving and investing half of your extra earnings and spending the other half on yourself. I say this over and over but I think it's so important to reward yourself. This is what will motivate you to continue to work hard and longevity is of the utmost importance to succeed in the long term.

Why Owning Your Home is Important

If you've read other financial books, blogs, or magazines you've most likely read about writers talking about the benefits of both renting and owning a home. I'll go through the basics points and then make a case as to why your end goal should be to own your own place and to have your mortgage paid off eventually.

The Benefits of Renting
There are benefits of renting. In a high interest environment, it's extremely expensive to own a home especially compared to what you could rent with an identical amount that you could pay in rent. A mortgage for a similar place is usually higher than rent would be, obviously with a variety of factors such as the size of your down payment. Owning a home will generally cost more across the board. You also won't need a down payment, which means you won't need a huge amount of cash in order to buy a place.

Renting makes it hassle-free as you don't have to worry about the upkeep about your place, the landlord will take care of all that. You don't have to pay for maintenance, property taxes, strata fees, and other pesky monthly fees that come along with home ownership. Insurance costs may be lower but you still want insurance for your personal belongings even as a tenant.

You also don't have any obligations to stay in your place. If you don't like your neighbor, the area you live in, or just don't like the place in general, once your lease is up (if you have one) you can give your one-month notice and just leave. Renting in general is much easier and less of a headache in comparison to home ownership.

The Benefits of Home Ownership
With all those benefits of renting, I might have you sold, but don't jump the gun just yet. Owning a home has its benefits too. By owning a home and paying your mortgage you are making an investment in your own home. Property prices generally do go up and unless something drastic like the Subprime collapse happens again, this trend will continue in the long term. You just have to use some common sense. Have property prices in your area climbed steadily or have them doubled in the last 5 years? If they've doubled in the past 5 years what are the chances of it continuing the climb? I'm not saying it can't happen but it could make it harder to continue climbing.

It's always been the American dream to own your own home, it's a sense of pride that you have. Having friends over and telling them it's really your place is something to be proud about. Obviously, this shouldn't be your main reason to own a home but it definitely doesn't hurt either.

All this is wonderful and in the short term it really depends on your cash flow and what you want out of the place you live. Everyone has different wants and needs.

Some want to live in the downtown core for a couple years and save up before they buy a place in the suburbs while some want to live in the downtown core forever. You need to have an idea as to what you want to do in 5-10 years range. I honestly think the 5 year range is sufficient as you could most likely buy a place now and if markets behave as they should under normal circumstances, you should have a decent return on your investment in your residence and in 5 years you'll most likely have had a few raises to be able to sustain a bigger mortgage when you buy a bigger and better home.

The biggest difference lies in the future. 20-30 years down the road when you are approaching retirement, if you've been good with your finances, you'll have paid off your mortgage. That means that you won't have any mortgage payments to worry about. Sure you'll have maintenance fees or strata fees if you live in a condo or town house, but these fees will be significantly less than if you own a home.

This means that you will have that much more breathing room in your retirement to do other things like travelling which you will most likely want to do. If you continue to rent into your retirement, you'll strand up a large portion of your retirement funds in something you could have planned for much earlier. If you have the cash sitting around now, the smartest move is to therefore buy a place and help yourself in the future while making a smart investment.

Thinking of your home as a Savings Plan

Every mortgage payment that you make is like a forced savings plan. Most people only think about how much it costs to own a home and how much of you can really afford in terms of your cash flow. And while this is the reality of a mortgage, you should look beyond that and think of how each mortgage payment will build your equity.

A mortgage payment consists of principal and interest. You should think of the interest as rent and the principal as an automatic savings plan. Essentially with every payment you make, you're building equity in your home, and this equity is what can make you wealthy especially if you principal residence is the biggest purchase in your life and for many people this is the case.

This is the biggest argument that is used for those that believe that owning a home is the best investment. While I think this is definitely true, take it with a grain of salt because it honestly depends on where in the world you live.

Why sometimes it makes sense to rent instead of owning a home

Housing prices are inflated in some parts of the world that buying a home can actually make you house rich and cash poor. This means that your mortgage payments are so big that you have little money to do anything else with. If this is this the case then renting a place within your means and investing the difference may put you well ahead of where you would be when you forced yourself into a corner just to be able to own a home.

The problem with this argument is that most people that rent aren't putting away the difference into an investment. The excess cash is used for other things like eating out, more clothes and things that really aren't helping your financial future. If you're going the renting route, then you need to be disciplined and plan out how you are going to be spending the difference between a mortgage payment and rent. I say this because for a similar place, you'll most likely have to eat into your savings for the down payment and the mortgage payment will most definitely be higher. If the mortgage payment, monthly strata fees, and other maintenance costs combined is lower than your monthly rent, then it's a no-brainer that you should be a home owner.

To get back on track, if you're saving $400 a month by renting. Then you need to focus on what you're doing with that $400 every month. To put things into perspective. Over 15 years, by putting away that $400 every month at a 6% annual return, you'll be adding an extra $116,327.49 to your retirement fund. That's nothing to sneeze at.

Even if you were to put half of that away, you could get over $58,000. That's a pretty sizeable amount. So spend some time and think about what your current financial situation is. How much are you paying for rent? How much do you have saved for a down payment? Can you buy a place now? If so, how much will your projected mortgage payment, maintenance fees, and added costs of owning your place be? Don't know? Then it's time you found out!

Life Stages

Everyone is in a different life stage. You could be coming right out of school and just starting your new job, already have a decent job and starting to settle down, or you might be going into retirement or are already retired. Whatever stage you are in, it's extremely important that you recognize the life stage that you are in and formulate your financial plan accordingly.

Getting Started Phase

In this phase, you're just getting out of school and most likely got your first job. You may or may not have student debt and might have bought your first car. You're excited to break into the real job world and want to start trying all sorts of things! It's an extremely exciting time but most people at this stage don't have a lot of money, obviously depending on the profession you're in.

At this stage in life, it's extremely difficult to figure out what to do with your money. You'll most likely make ~~some~~ many dumb mistakes both financially and socially. But that's ok, as long as you don't over do it. That's how we all learn, make your mistakes while it's still socially ok for you to make those mistakes. It's the same with financial mistakes. You want to make those mistakes early in life but don't dig yourself too big a hole because if you do, it can get extremely hard to get out of. Let's look at some very important factors when you're starting out.

Building your Credit Score

Focus on building your credit, not destroying it. As a banker, I have seen many people starting with horrible credit. Some might have derogatory or items in collections which absolute destroy their credit. Don't think that it's ok to have horrible credit early on in life because credit is something that can be extremely difficult to build back up. If you have collection items, it can take 7 years to drop off and that's a very long time, especially if you are looking to buy your own home.

Buying Your First Car

The next big mistake that many people starting out make is buy a brand new car that is most likely out of their means. Sure you want to look good and have a great ride. But when you're starting out and have loans to pay back and have more bills like rent, groceries and all that, the extra $500-700 a month between your car loan payment, gas, insurance, and maintenance can really take a dent into your budget. If you must have a car, try and buy used. You can actually get great used car deals. Don't buy from shady car dealers and buy from legitimate car dealerships if you have a choice. Buy from Craigslist or other places at your own risk, sure you might get an even better deal, but you have to ask yourself if it's really worth the risk.

Setting Your Monthly Budget

We've already talked about creating a budget, but I can't stress how important it is for you at this stage. At this stage in life there are so many temptations. Your friends will be asking you out, you'll be going on dates, buying new clothes, taking vacations, and much more. You'll easily be able to spend all the money you earn. I'm a huge fan of experiencing as much as you can in life.

Again, the more mistakes and bad experiences in life you have at an early stage the better the person you'll be.

As a side note, there are so many douchebag men and snotty women in this world. I don't care how much you make or who you think you are, be humble. Being a douchebag or being snotty will only get you so far. If you think you're better than someone else, well guess what, there will <u>always</u> be someone that is better than you are. Be humble and be yourself. Learn to love yourself and learn to love those around you. Try and make the world a better place. You'll feel better about yourself. Trust me.

Getting back on track, keep track of your expenses for a couple months at least preferable longer. In this day in age, you should be able to log into your online banking and see what you did with your bank account and your credit card. Make yourself a decent cup of coffee and spend some time analyzing your spending. This is extremely important; remember saving and investing a small amount regularly can put you ahead big time. Think of your future. Financial discipline is extremely important and you want to develop those habits as soon as you possibly can.

The Accumulation Phase
At this point, you've most likely been working for a few years and have paid off your student debt, have established your credit a little bit and have started to put money aside for your rainy day and have some investments. Your career is doing ok and you might even be considering buying your own place in the near future. It's an exciting time, but it can be scary because you might have big dreams and goals and your current state might not be exactly where you want to be. I've been

through this stage and trust me, it gets better but you have to be diligent and create a plan that you can stick to.

Buying Your First Home

Ah, the American dream of buying your first home. Unless you want to rent for the rest of your life, you want to buy your home. I've given both arguments for and against buying a home in a previous chapter because I want you to make an informed decision and at the end of the day it really comes down to personal preference. But I think you should buy just because of all of the benefits down the road. Put it this way, regardless of the return that you get on your place in the form of capital appreciation, or the value of your home going up, you need a place to live. And once you pay off your mortgage in 25-30 years, guess what? You won't have any more mortgage payments. I hope you realize how much this could help your retirement. As you'll only have to worry about maintenance, property taxes and some other minor stuff. If you keep renting, you'll have to rent forever and most likely won't be able to upgrade the place you rent.

We talked about how there are numbers out there that tell you that you might be better off renting and investing you money rather than simply buying. While this might be true, I want you to think of it in your own situation. Let's say you invested $500,000 in the stock market and saw your money grow by 75% to $875,000! The question is, would you be able to hold onto your investments for that long? Or would you take your money and run with the profits when you had a 30%, 40%, or even 50% return?

The same can be said about your home purchase. Let's say you buy a place for $500,000 and it goes up in value to $875,000! The same 75% gain in price. But the difference is, you won't be able to take profits with your property with a click of a button or by visiting your branch. Selling a home can be a much more painful and stressful experience, and this will deter you from selling your home unless you have enough saved and want to buy a better place. Most people don't watch the value of their home fluctuate on a daily basis, because they can't.

But many people watch how the market performs and when someone is up 30-40% in their investment portfolio, they look at the dollar figure and cash in, only to watch the market keep going up. So don't let those numbers deceive you. Unless you can completely ignore your investment portfolio for 20 years, the reality will very different.

So now that I've convinced you to buy your own home, you need to think about saving for your down payment. The more you save the better it is, to give you an idea as to how things work in Canada. You need 20% down in order to avoid any default insurance that you need to pay for extra through companies like CMHC. But that shouldn't stop you from buying a home if you can afford it. There are many people that buy a place with 5% down, you just have to do the numbers, although if you have anything less than 5% down, the numbers have to work because the banks will tell you straight up if they don't.

If you able to qualify for your mortgage, which you should do before you begin your home search by getting a mortgage pre-approval from your own bank (or shop around), then that's what you should base your search on.

The down payment will be the hardest part as you start off with your accumulation phase. Talk to your banker to see how much you really need as a competent banker should be able to tell you how much you need. But do your own research and look for comparable properties to what you currently rent and see if you can afford something similar in the same area. Don't forget to consider maintenance or strata fees, property taxes, and other upkeep you will incur as a homeowner. Always overbudget!

Adding to your Investment Portfolio
You need to know what your number is for retirement and for other goals you have in life. If you need a million dollars before you retire, what does that look like in terms of putting money away every paycheck? Spend some time to do your calculations. Think about how many years you have before you can retire. If you're 30 years old and want to retire at the age of 60, then you have 30 years. If you wanted to invest every paycheck which is every two weeks and are expecting a 6% return, you'd need to stash away roughly $444.30 every 2 weeks for 30 years. That doesn't sound too bad now does it? But you have to consistently do that for 30 years.

Is a million dollars enough? Again, it depends. If you can continue to have the 6% return in retirement, then without depleting your capital, you'll be getting a $60,000 before tax income from your investments. That's not bad by any means, but if you need $80,000 after tax funds to live off of you'll be short. So you'll need to compromise something. Either invest more regularly, extend your timeframe before you retire, or strive to lower your living standards in retirement, which should be very different from your lifestyle at the age of 30.

We talk about the importance of regular contributions as well as making the contributions automatic. At this stage in life, it's very important to automate the contributions and make it a necessary obligation. Think of it as another bill that must be paid. Can you skip your rent, hydro, car loan payment? I hope not. Well, the automatic contribution that you make should be in the same category and something you need to make on an ongoing basis.

Much like the starting out phase, there are a lot of temptations in this phase too. Now that you have a little more money, you want to go on an extravagant vacation, maybe take a year sabbatical, buy a nicer car, and more. But the reality is, if you do any of these things it's gong to set you back unless you saved for these things separately, which I do recommend.

The accumulation phase is important because whatever you do here will affect your retirement phase. Find the right balance between having fun (which you should definitely do!) and putting money aside. If you like working than maybe you don't need to retire so early, but if you want to enjoy life outside the workplace later in life, then it might be important to stash more money away.

Retirement Phase
So the day has come that you've spent 30 years at your company or are self-employed and are selling your company to a third-party and it's time to enjoy life after work. Congratulations! You now get to bear the fruit of all

your hard work. It should be a great feeling when you hit this stage.

But be careful, I've seen many people that hit this stage and have no idea what to do with all of their free time. So some planning needs to take place in that regard too. You were working between 9-5 plus commuting time and now all of a sudden you have all this time on your hands, you better find something to do so you don't drive yourself and those around you crazy!

In the retirement phase you need to revisit your expenses once more. Everything will change since you're not working anymore and your priorities will lie elsewhere. You probably won't be paying as much for transportation since you're not commuting anymore. You might be paying less for clothing because you don't need to dress up for work. If you still have a mortgage, this could go down now that you have an empty nest at home with all your children having moved out, you could downgrade your home and have that extra cash on hand and invest it.

Going into retirement is a huge life event and you should be planning for this day well in advance because if you don't, you will be in for a rude awakening. So many books talk about how to save for retirement but not what to do in retirement. Saving for retirement shouldn't be that hard and I hope I'm getting that point across to you in this book. If you start early and are diligent with your savings and actually invest your money then you give yourself a very solid chance to have ample money and potentially leave a legacy for your children and grandchildren. Now doesn't that sound nice?

I have seen many GIC investors. While I can't blame them, many of them are so stubborn beyond saving, and I pray and hope you aren't one of them. GICs or Guaranteed Investment Certificates are what banks and other financial institutions sell for a set interest rate for whatever period you choose. I think as a kid you hear from you parents all the time how important it is to put money away in GICs!

There virtually is no risk with GICs unless you're buying from a shady institution. But if you go to your large bank, then there should be no risk. What people fail to realize is that while your principal and the interest may not be at risk, there is other risk involved and that is inflation risk and therefore purchasing power risk.

When you put money in a GIC especially in a low interest environment, like the one we're going through now at the time of writing this book in 2013, you might get 1% on your GIC. Now history has inflation at 3% in Canada (interest rate and inflation rate will vary according to the country) and as you can see for every year that you keep your money in a GIC, you're losing purchasing power. Purchasing power is the ability to buy the same good with your money. So that means that if buy a chocolate bar $1.00 today, with inflation it will be $1.03 next year, but your investment return is only 1%, so you won't have enough money to buy the chocolate bar next because you only have $1.01.

I hope you understand that it's important to take some risk with your investments now. You cannot possibly expect to retire early if you aren't willing to take some risk for the potential of higher returns. Now, just because you take more risk doesn't necessarily mean you will get a higher return. What it does mean is that you give yourself a better chance of achieving a higher return.

So let's look at a couple scenarios.

Scenario 1: Zoheb has $100,000 to invest, wants to invest only in GICs but wants enough money for retirement. In our current interest rate environment Zoheb would only be able to get around 1% but let's be generous and give her 2.5%. Zoheb has 25 years until retirement and reinvests the money every year.

With these figures, the investor would have $185,394.40. That's an 85.4% increase over 25 years, not bad for not taking any risk. But don't forget there's inflation and well you do have to pay taxes on those returns too...

Scenario 2: Steve has the same $100,000 but is willing to take some risk and is willing to buy a Balanced Fund, which has mix of cash, fixed income, and equities or stocks. The average projected rate of return is 7% and Steve also has 25 years until retirement.

For Steve, his funds will turn into $542,743.26 after 25 years. That's nearly triple of what Zoheb has after 25 years and would be 542.7% return over 25 years. This is without any extra contributions! Do you see the difference now?

Don't get caught up in the risk of returns. That's a trap many people fall into. Think about the risk of not having enough and the risk of how inflation and taxes eat into your returns. This is the real risk that you should be focusing on. Over time risk averages out and when you think long term (10+ years) you will be fine even when you invest in the stock market. Even with the horrific fall in 2008, the markets have recovered since and you would be past breakeven, and in fact better than holding GICs over that period. Learn to live with risk. We'll talk more about this in a later chapter.

Leaving a Legacy for your Loved Ones
Many people want to leave something behind for their loved ones. By planning well in ahead, you have the chance to do this too. Everyone has a different view for leaving a legacy, but it could come in the form of your home, or leaving a portion of your investment portfolio. Some people leave nothing and it all comes down to your values for this. Whatever you decide is honestly fine but if you do decide to leave something, let's look at one option.

Many financial planners will help you determine the number that you need to retire and have ample income in retirement. However, what these financial planners do is have you come up with a number that will deplete your investment by the time you die. And with the longevity nowadays, sometimes what you have in your investment portfolio will not be enough.

Let's look at an example.

Rick determines that he will need $50,000 a year in retirement. Rick is currently 25 years old and plans to retire at the age of 55. So he has 30 years before he retires and plans to live until he is 85. So that means he has 30 years in retirement as well. Many financial planners would determine what Rick would need until the age of 85. So in this case, at 5% return post-retirement this number would be $768,622.55. What this number represents is what Rick would need to have saved by the age of 55, but by the time he is 85 he will have absolutely nothing left in his investment account meaning he will leave nothing for his loved ones.

Now to dig a little deeper with Rick's situation, let's say he gets a 7% annual return pre-retirement for the 30 years and starts with zero investment. This means he would need to save $630 a month to reach this goal. Whether if you think this is a big amount will depend on your income and cash flow situation, but the fact of the matter is to achieve a $50,000 annual retirement income it's really not that bad. Think of it this way, you're putting away $630 a month for 30 years to get $4,167 ($50,000/12 months) for 30 years. Now doesn't that seem like a pretty good deal? I think it does.

What if Rick wanted to leave his entire investment portfolio for his loved ones? This means that instead of having the investment portfolio getting depleted at 85, he needs to be able to get the $50,000 annual income without having his investment portfolio getting depleted. Sounds like a daunting task doesn't it? Not really, let's dig a little deeper.

Using the same 5% post-retirement return, to achieve $50,000 a year Rick would need an investment portfolio of $1,000,000. That's only $231,377.45 more than his initial plan. Sure it's a big number but let's see what that translates to over 30 years.

At the same 7% pre-retirement return for 30 years, that's an extra of about $190 per month. So that's a total of $630+$190=$820 per month to reach the magic $1,000,000 number. Now Rick can meet his living standards and leaving a legacy for his loved ones. On a side note, the Rick I know would likely need a lot more with all the expensive clothes, extravagant vacations, and food that he eats...but that's another story.

Now another point I want to talk about is the pre-retirement and post-retirement returns. The reason your post-retirement return should be lower is because you want to take less risk in retirement relatively to your pre-retirement years. Why? Because before you retire, you're working and have a solid income coming in and can mitigate the risk that you're taking. But once you retire, you're dependent on the return that your investment portfolio provides and thus want to lower the risk.

Planning Your Expenses Out
Regardless of the life stage you're in, it's very important to look at your expenses and cash flow. This is especially true in retirement since you have limited income earning potential. Your expenses should go down but this isn't the case for everyone and some people like to travel more and do things they never were able to before. Everything adds up and that's why it's important to stick to the budget that you have. Like in Rick's case, if he said $50,000 is enough then he needs to stick to that plan otherwise he'll likely start depleting his funds.

In retirement, it's important to dissect your expenses on an annual and monthly level. On an annual level, think about what you'll be spending money on over the year. The property taxes and maintenance of your home, vacations you'll be going on during the year, any gifts you'll be buying, etc. On a monthly level look at your daily expenses as you always have so that you don't go over your budget and you're conscious of where you should be.

Plan, plan, and plan some more!
Regardless of the life stage that you are in, remember that you need to plan. The earlier you start and the more you stash away, the easier it is. There's no need for you to panic or get uneasy about any of this. Don't let the details scare you. With a solid plan, you just put money away on a consistent basis hopefully diversified properly and you'll do just fine. Let your trusted investment professional deal with the rest. I do recommend sticking with the larger financial institutions and I'll talk about this somewhere else in this book. You should be reading the whole book so I'll let you search for it!

Remember be disciplined and stick to your plan. Creating a plan is one thing, but actually taking action is another. This is the case with anything in life. Good luck!

Section 2: Saving & Investing for your Future

Save For Your Rainy Day!

Do you have a rainy day fund? If you don't now's a good time to start. It doesn't matter how organized you are with your finances and how well your investments are doing, there are unexpected events that happen to each and every one of us. The Rainy Day fund is your emergency fund to dip into in the case that something happens. Sure you might have funds saved elsewhere, but why would you want to eat into your vacation savings when you and delay your luxurious vacation to Hawaii when you could prepare for your rainy day properly.

How Much is Enough?
That's the big question, how much is enough? The general consensus seems to be 3-6 months living expenses. I personally go for 3 months living expenses while others may prefer 6 months. It really depends on every individual's comfort zone. If you have liquid investments such as cashable term deposit or decent cash flow every month from passive investments that you don't depend on, (for example, dividends from stocks), then you might not need such a big amount stashed away.

If you have a line of credit at your bank are comfortable with borrowing a little bit, then you could also limit how much you have in your Rainy Day fund. It all comes down to what you are comfortable with and how risk tolerant you are. Usually, risk tolerance is tested with investing, but I firmly believe that everything we do in life involves risk. If you aren't comfortable with something, that simply means that you aren't comfortable with the risk involved. Think of the Rainy Day fund as insurance for your living expenses, only this is insurance that you provide for yourself, and it's free!

How do you Save For it?
So the next question is, how do you save for your rainy day fund when you already have all the expenses you worry about? The answer to this is to pay yourself first. When you get your paycheck, either setup automatic transfers to a dedicated account for your rainy day funds or do it manually before using money for anything else. The key is to treat your rainy day fund contribution as a fixed expense that you must put money into. Think of it as an electricity bill, without any electricity you can't survive, your rainy day fund is your backup electricity source.

Where Do You Keep Your Rainy Day Funds

Once you're ready to put funds away you need to decide where to house the funds. The key is to keep your money somewhere very liquid. The definition of liquid here is that they can be turned into cash almost immediately when you need the funds.

The easiest way is to open a savings account at the bank you deal with already. If you're like me, you simply open up your account through Internet banking, it's really that simple. Just log in and you should be able to open a Savings account. The key here is to find the account with absolutely no fees and pays you an interest for keep any balance, even if it's only one dollar. You do not want an account that eats into your savings for any reason.

Do some shopping around too, there are some places where you can open an account online and keep money there, just make sure your aren't putting your money somewhere that isn't safe. No, I wouldn't trust some shady website on the other side of the world offering 94.7% monthly interest. Be reasonable and use some common sense please!

Another great place to keep your money are cashable GICs (Guaranteed Investment Certificates) that you can invest through your bank or credit union. Just make sure you look at the interest rates and the terms and conditions. Some cashable GICs look great at first glance since you can take your money out at anytime, but some of them won't pay you a penny of interest if you take your money out too early. And well interest rates are pretty dismal in the past few years so check the rates!

There are variety of other options but just make sure it's safe and you can get your money asap when you need it.

When do you Use Your Rainy Day Fund?

It might be a good idea for you to define what is a rainy day for you. For some, running out of lollipops or having no money for beer might be a grave emergency. But for our purposes, we need to think about what could really hurt our finances when something a little more important hits.

Here are some Rainy Day Events:
- Your car breaks down and you need a new engine
- You child has an emergency of some sort
- You lose your job without any notice
- ~~You find a beautiful pair of shoes on sale~~, nice try ladies.

Our lives are filled with unexpected events. Sometimes that's a good thing, you meet great people, you find great deals, or you're just plain lucky. But sometimes something horrible can happen that you have absolutely no control over. These are the times that you need to dip into your rainy day fund. And remember, if you use part or all of your rainy day fund you need to replenish it again in case something happens again in the future. It's all about being financially smart and sound. Don't be stupid!

Create a Bank Account for Everything!

When people hear that I have 9 bank accounts, they think I'm crazy. Why on Earth would you need 9 bank accounts? You only need one checking account and one savings account right? Sure for the majority of people, this might suffice but for me and for you who's reading this book, it isn't enough. Let's look at why.

I've already talked about saving for your purchases before actually buying the item. This can't always be the case as we know, especially for bigger purchases like a car or a house. But for the rest of the things we want in life this is the mindset you want to have. And just so you know, your credit card limit and line of credit limits are not considered spendable savings!

I have one main checking account that all of my transactions go through. All of my bill payments including hydro, rent/mortgage, credit card payments, ATM and debit transactions go through this account. I then have one US account, as I live in Canada, to keep US funds so that I don't lose out on the exchange rate or can take advantage of the exchange rate when I have extra cash and plan to go to the US in the near future.

The 7 other accounts are savings accounts that I use for a variety of purposes. My bank allows me to nickname each account and so I do that. Every paycheck that I get, I have a set amount of funds that go into each account and they accumulate interest on a monthly basis as well. Here are the 7 accounts that I have, you can mix and match or have other accounts as needed. They're all free accounts by the way.

The Leisure Account
This is where I budget my leisure activities. Whether if it's going out for drinks or dinner, hobbies, or anything else that's fun. I put funds in this account so that I can tap into this account every time I do something that's "leisure" related.

The Big Purchase Fund
Other than a car or house, all of my big purchases I do my absolute best to save for. If I'm buying an instrument, a new computer, or something that's a luxury item I save money for it first and start looking when I'm closing to reaching the monetary value of the item in question. Never go shopping for an item if you aren't close to it, we all fall into the trap of thinking that we found the best deal possible (when you can't afford it) only to find out a week later there is an even better sale on.

Vacation Fund
This is pretty self-explanatory. Whether if you go on a vacation once a year or every 2 months, you should be setting aside funds from each paycheck to cover the

vacations that you go on. People always talk about having to worry about their credit card bill when they come back from a vacation. Don't be one of those irresponsible people, save for the vacation as much as you can before you actually go on the vacation, trust me, you'll thank me later.

The Gift Account
This is a fund that I throw money into just like any other account. It's for birthday and Christmas presents for the most part. But it's also a fund that I dip into when I want to thank someone or just simply give someone a gift. A small gift can go a long way, and having the funds for it helps you quite a bit too. Showing a little gratitude never hurts.

The Clothing Fund
We all need to buy clothing and if clothing isn't your big thing, you can rename this to a hobby or something that you spend money on somewhat regularly. People can buy clothes endlessly, even men. You can spend an infinite amount of clothes but this is my way of controlling my spending by making sure I have enough saved up for it.

So how do you determine how much you put into each account? That depends entirely on how much you earn. You obviously don't want to over do it, and these accounts are all luxury accounts, accounts that don't make a part of your necessities. The first thing you do when you get your paycheck is look at the necessities you have to keep living. Your rent/mortgage, any fixed expenses you might have such as food, strata fees, child care, and education.

Your savings and investments should be your next priority. How much are you stashing away of your pay? Is it 10%? Then you look at things like car payments, insurance, other somewhat necessities such as cable, internet, cell phone and other things depending on what you do such as gym expenses.

With the remaining funds, you then decide on how you will disperse each remaining dollar. I like to use percentages of your pay rather than using arbitrary dollar figures, just because if your pay grows, so will the amount you put into each account. That way you can break down your pay easier without having to dwell on a round dollar figure.

I hope this helps you organize your finances a little better. You could take this a step further and write down some of the goals that you have for each fund. If it's a big purchase fund, what are some of the things you want to buy? How about your clothing fund? Sounds like fun doesn't it? Just make sure you don't spend too much time "researching" your next big purchase, because it can be a little tempting to just buy it now!

The Power of Time and The Power of Compounding

Whatever reason you have behind saving money, you need to understand what compounding is and how it will help you achieve your goals. This is one of those occasions that time will actually be on your side. Unlike when you borrow money, interest rates will also be on your side and my hope is that this will entice you to save more money for the long term.

Compounding is very simple. If you put money away now, your investment will get interest or a return regularly and if you reinvest those new funds, you will get interest on those extra funds. This goes on until you take money out of this investment and the longer you can keep your money invested, the more you will have to spend when the time comes when you actually need the money.

Let's do a simple calculation to illustrate the power of compounding. Henry just got a $500 monthly raise (lucky him!) and wants to invest these funds separately to buy a luxury car in his retirement.

So here are the criteria for the calculation:
Years until retirement: 30 years
Projected Interest Annual Return on Investment: 5%
Monthly Investment: $500

In the first scenario, we'll look at how much he will have if he did not compound his investment. This simply means that he is getting a 5% return and not reinvesting those funds. So at the end of the 30 years he would be left with only the initial investment without any return because he would taken any returns out of the investment immediately upon getting it.

The calculation would be 30 years x 12 months x $500 = $180,000.
So as you can see, that's still a pretty nice amount of money and he could probably buy most luxury cars. Of course the sky is the limit with cars but he could a pretty decent super car for that amount, even in 30 years! The

annual return on investment would be around $300, so over 30 years we're looking at an extra $9,000.

So let's now look at the power of compounding with the same criteria, this time reinvesting all returns. By reinvesting all returns and having an annual return of 5% with $500 being invested monthly, Henry would have $416,129.32!

So to get my point across again, by using compounding you can grow your investment significantly faster. The key is not only to use compounding but also to keep adding to your investment, which only increases the speed at which your investment will grow. If you make contributions on a weekly or monthly basis it won't hurt your wallet all that much but before you know it, you'll see a huge difference in your investments.

The Power of Passive Income

Wouldn't it be great if you could wake up every morning and not have to worry about driving out to some job to earn your living? We all dream about it, and that's the goal you should have in mind. It might not happen overnight unless you win the lottery, but if you work at it, you'll get there. It's all about having the right mindset and sticking to your plan.

Saving money is one thing, creating a passive source of income is another. Passive income is any source of income that requires minimal time input. It means that you money will show up in your bank account without you having to think or work too much. It's the best form of income! Passive income is the type of income you should strive to increase, because once your passive income surpasses your expenses, you don't have to work. Now doesn't that sounds like something to work towards?

It's obviously easier said than done since passive income requires a lot more work to achieve that regular income. Regular income, you get a job, put your time and you get a paycheck. For passive income, you either need to invest a lot or be creative.

Here are some examples of passive income:
Dividends – from either a Public or Private company
Rent from Real Estate
Earnings from a business that require you to do very little
Royalties – From book sales, Intellectual Property, music, etc.
Earning money from advertisements on websites or blogs
Pension Income

There are other sources and your imagination is what will be key here. A very common source of income is dividends from public companies. You simply buy shares of companies that pay a dividend and you've created a source of passive income. It's one of the most stable ways to make money since you'll be able to increase the amount you get paid at anytime, given that you have the money to add to your investments. Sure the stock market can be scary, but if you're smart about it then you won't be worried about what the stock market does. Dividends can be paid on a monthly, quarterly, semi-annual, or annual basis.

In some countries, dividend income has great tax benefits as well. In Canada, there is something called a dividend tax credit resulting in less taxes paid on dividend income in comparison to regular income, for example employment or interest income. Check with your tax advisor to see if you get any benefits for investing in dividend paying stocks in your country.

Rental income is also a great source of income. Real estate investments can be tough and you will need a relatively large amount of capital to invest in real estate especially with the credit crunch since 2008, but there are great deals out there that you can buy and rent for a profit. Just remember with real estate, location is everything. But just because you have a property in a great location doesn't mean you can overpay for a property. The more you pay, the less profit you will have. And then there's the headache of finding and dealing with tenants. However, the rewards can be amazing if you can work it out.

Business income that requires little of your time is a strong source of income. You could buy a business that already generates a positive cash flow with little extra work needed or you could build your business from scratch. It all depends on you and your financial standing. If you can afford to buy a business and are confident with valuing and running one, then this might be the great source of passive income for you. Just remember the rate of business failures are high, especially start-ups.

Royalties are another great source of passive income. By me writing this book, I will be getting royalties for every book that sells. Although I have to put a significant amount of time to write this book, it's a one-time investment that will hopefully turn into a strong source of passive income. If you can invent something that is in demand that is intellectual property that you will be able to have a patent for which is another source of passive income. And of course, if you can become a rockstar all of your music will become a source of passive income.

Earning money from advertisements on websites is also a form of passive income. Of course, it depends on how much time you spend on creating the website. If it is an ongoing part time job to keep the website growing and running, then it really isn't passive income. But if you can figure out a way to make it run automatically, such as having a forum where contributors to the forum will create content automatically, this is a great source of passive income. However, this is much easier said than done as the competition for having a popular website/blog/forum is extreme.

Wherever you are in the world, when you retire most likely the government will provide you with pension income that will supplement your retirement funds. Some companies will also have a good pension plan to add to this. You should find out how much the government and the company you work for will provide in your retirement. This will vary drastically depending on your income level as well as number of years worked at the company, among other factors. I personally look at this as a bonus and don't intend on relying on pension income to help me too much in retirement and you shouldn't either. Focus on building wealth so that you have full control of how much you have in retirement.

As you can see, there are a variety of forms of passive income. Some will be better suited to your personality than others. Some may be wonderful writers that can write best sellers one after another, while others will be great business owners. You don't need to have all forms of passive income. Some successful individuals will focus on one form and be wealthier than most can imagine. I think it's ideal to have two or three forms of passive income in case one of them doesn't do too well. If you want to retire early, you should focus on building your passive income. This is the key to financial freedom.

The 50/50 Rule. The Importance of Rewarding Yourself every time you Save Money

Saving money definitely isn't as easy as spending money. That's why when you save money, you should reward yourself every time. The 50/50 rule has you saving 50% of your savings towards your savings for a goal while the other 50% goes to money that you can spend on anything you like.

Another good way to look at saving money is that a dollar saved is two dollars earned. Sure we aren't all in the highest marginal tax bracket, but assuming that you pay taxes in one way or another, it's a good mindset to have when you are saving money. Every dollar you save is actually saving you two dollars because of the taxes.

Once you start to get on a roll of saving money it's really easy to get caught up on saving more and more. It can be fun but for many it can also become an obsession. Remember, your goal is to be frugal, not be cheap. Save money with a goal and purpose but also spend your savings on things that you really want to buy and that money can be spent on luxury items, vacations, extravagant dinners and more.

Focus on the Type of Return and Not the Return Itself

The return of an investment is important. 9% is always better than 5% right? Is it really? It depends on a variety of factors including the tax bracket you're in and the type of return that we're looking at. For this, you need to spend some time looking at the tax laws of the area/country you live in because it will be different depending on where you live.

In Canada, we have quite a few ways in which distributions are taxed. If we start talking about corporations and trusts it gets even more complicated so I'll stick to how we're taxed on a personal level. Simply put, for investments we are taxed for regular income, interest, eligible dividends, capital gains, and return of capital.

Interest and regular income are taxed at the same level and so every dollar you earn at your 9-5 job or the interest you earn on your Guaranteed Interest Certificate (GIC) is taxed the same way, at the worst and highest rate possible. The next step down is eligible dividends and these are dividends of stocks of public and private companies, you'll need to check if the dividends that are being paid fit in this category.

Don't get dividends mixed up with eligible dividends. Just because a stock or income trust is paying a dividend, don't assume it is an eligible dividend. Many Real Estate Investment Trusts, trusts that are traded on stock markets and investment in real estate, give you a distribution that are classified as "dividends" but if you look at the actual distribution aren't always eligible dividends.

To get back on track, capital gains are the gains you have from an investment. If you buy a stock and make $1,000 because the stock price when up, that's a capital gain. In Canada, capital gains are taxed at the lowest tax rate. Return of Capital is something you see with some mutual funds. This is as the name suggests where you are given a part of your initial investment back.

So to get back to the original question as to if 9% is always a better return than 5%, it isn't. If you had a 9% return of interest but only had a 5% return with capital gains, in terms of tax the end result is the same. This is at least the case in Canada. So like the old adage, never judge a cover by its book. Just because a mutual fund returned 5%, don't assume it did worse than the fund that had a 7.5% return. Take some time to look at the distributions.

This is especially true if you are in a higher tax bracket since you could be taxed painfully for every extra dollar you earn. If you get a $1,000 return on your investment, would you rather keep $750 of that or keep $660 of it? That's one example. And guess what, that $90 different will make or break your retirement fund and could equal to an extra year of work and delaying your retirement.

Depending on the country you live in, there are tax shelters. In Canada, we have the Registered Retirement

Savings Plan (RRSP) and Tax Free Savings Account (TFSA). By holding any investment inside these accounts you never have to worry about the distributions because you're never taxed at the time of the distribution. With the RRSP, you're taxed when you take the money out of the RRSP and with the TFSA you're never taxed period.

Why Mutual Funds aren't actually that bad

If you know me, you'll know that I hated mutual funds with a passion. Yes, hate. That's a very strong word, however I have started to change my opinion of mutual funds as time has passed. If you read around, you'll find many people share my old sentiment. So what brought about this change and why do I think you should include mutual funds in your Investment Portfolio?

First off, let's talk about what mutual funds are. I'm sure you've heard of them. When you visit a bank branch or watch the news you've most likely heard about the pros and cons of mutual funds. You've most likely heard of some horror stories with ponzi schemes like that of Bernard Madoff spending the money he should have been investing.

If you ignore the extremes, and focus on what mutual funds really are, they are a pool of funds with a mandate to invest in a certain way. Mutual funds are an immense industry and have grown exponentially and for good reason, mutual funds allow the average investor or non-investor to stick money in one of these trusts and forget about them. Well that is until something what happened in 2008 and you lose 49.7% of your initial investment value.

I never liked mutual funds because of how I thought fees were a big issue. I also didn't like that you had to pay taxes when you didn't realize any gains yourself. I also thought arrogantly that I could beat any mutual fund on a consistent basis.

However, after working for a bank I can tell you that some of these things depend. The fees for the mutual fund won't go away, it costs money to run these things and if a fund manager is doing a good job, then they deserve to get paid well. However, even if you were to do the investments yourself, it still costs money to buy and sell the individual securities. The taxes are either deferred or paid up front, and you honestly need not worry about the details because in the long run, it all averages out.

Not all mutual funds and mutual fund companies are made equal. If you're a bank hater, and I know there are a ton of bank haters, then you're most likely going to either blindly pick a smaller mutual fund company because you have this perception that a smaller firm can somehow beat a larger firm, or the fact that you just can't stand large banks and have this misconception that you'll get more attention if you go to a smaller firm.

Well, if this is your case, you'll be in for a rude awakening when you invest with a smaller brokerage or investment firm. Again, not all firms are made the same. Even within the same firm one client will get different services from another client. This is the case everywhere regardless of where you go. It could be the fact that you have more money in your account, your fund manager might like you more for whatever reason, or maybe you were one of the first clients.

When it comes to mutual fund companies, size often does matter. It's called economies of scale. Just think of Walmart and your local grocery store. Who do you think gets a better deal when they're buying from a supplier? You guessed it, Walmart does. The same goes for a large-scale mutual fund company. Their costs in general will be much lower for each dollar invested. When you have such high volume, you pay very little for your trade commissions as well as everything else.

To add to this, large firms will have a bigger team of analysts and fund managers. Unfortunately, this is where size and quantity don't matter. A small firm with a brilliant fund manager can potentially beat a fund company with 5 portfolio managers. It won't be easy though because the smaller company will likely charge a higher management fee because they have to in order to run their business. Smaller fund companies will have less funds under management which means they can only make so much money.

Let's use some real examples. A small fund company might have $150 million under management. Let's say they charge 3.5%, so that translates to $5.25 million in annual fees collected by the fund, this covers absolutely everything including the fund manager's salary. A large-scale bank has a similar fund with a similar mandate (think North American Equity Fund) but has a Management Expense Ratio (MER) of only 1.5% but has $30 billion under management. That translates to $450 million. The larger bank will likely have more expenses and more fund managers and bigger team of analysts.

But you can see that there's a 2% difference in the fees that you pay from your returns. In this case we are using an apples to apples comparison.

You might think that this isn't a realistic example. But the fact of the matter is, you'll find this example all over the investment industry. It's just how it is, and that's why you need to find a fund company that is transparent with their fees and don't charge your load fees when you buy or sell out of the fund. Be very careful of deferred sales charges that charge you a fee if you sell your holdings in a fund within a certain timeframe. It happens all the time.

What is Risk?

For any investment the success of that investment is measured in terms of the return that it produced. It really depends on the type of investment to determine if it performed well or not. You cannot be comparing the return of gold to the return of a stock. Well you can, but it really is comparing apples to oranges. Each investment is different and each investment has different risk.

You can read all you want but you'll never understand what risk is unless you ask yourself. This is because risk is a very relative term. What's risky to one person will be an entire different concept to someone else. Your risk tolerance level will be dependent on a number of variables such as income level, past experiences, knowledge, and investable assets. That's just to name a few. You might be fine investing in precious metals but be horrified of investing in GICs.

Risk also depends on all kinds of things including your income level, your age, your environment, the global economy, how the stock market is performing in general, and much more. When the markets are performing well, everyone has a high level of risk or they make themselves believing that they do.

You'll see people investing in stocks and when the market caps out and starts falling, everyone suddenly realizes that they actually weren't risk tolerant at all and might sell off everything or start praying that the market stops falling. These people should actually have been taking much less risk but because they didn't analyze themselves, they weren't able to figure out how much risk they were able to take.

Risk is very scary. Fund Managers are measured by the amount of return that they produce and not necessarily by the amount of risk that they take. A fund manager that produces a 15% return on any year (unless the market benchmark was 25% or any number higher than 15%), is considered amazing. This is especially true if he or she can do this on a consistent basis. Just think about how great that really is. If we were to use the rule of 72, whereby if you have a consistent return consistently (in this case 15%) and divide that by 72, you would get 4.8. That means that every 4.8 years you would double your money. With a track record like that that fund manager would be considered on the best of the best.

But what if I told you that in order for this fund manager to achieve that 15% return, he's taking risks to the point that he could potentially lose 50% of his fund every year. He was just lucky in the fact that the worst-case scenario, which the fund manager hopefully envisioned, didn't occur. This is something you likely won't see as this is behind the scenes information. The fund manager would never want you to know how much risk he is taking, in fact most likely most fund managers are unable to quantify exactly how much risk they are taking.

The same goes for your personal investments. When you buy the stock of Pfizer or Apple, do you really know how much risk you are taking? Do you know how much you are willing to lose? I doubt it, you're probably spending most of your time thinking about how much money you'll be able to make it. Back in September 2012 when Apple hit $700 a share, analysts were calling for an eventual $1,000 per share. I mean it went all the way up to $700 what's another $300 right?

Well, soon thereafter the stock started to fall. Come April 2013, the stock is below $400. That's a 43% drop. Just imagine yourself investing $100,000 and watching that drop to $57,000. Can you stomach that? Sure you might have gotten out somewhere earlier. But would you have? Most people freeze and pray to the gods that the market will find support, settle and then make it's way all the way back.

Mind you, if something falls 43%, you need the market to go back up by much more than 43%. A 43% return from $400 is only $572. You actually need a 75% move to the upside to make up for the lost ground. Same dollar value at $300, but hugely different return needed to recuperate your losses.

So before you start talking about how much risk you're willing to take at the next cocktail party, spend some quality time thinking about what risk means to you.

For me, it depends on what we're talking about. I always tell my friends that on a scale of 1 to 10, my risk tolerance is an 18. Yes you read that right, I'm extremely risk tolerant. But this is because I've spent countless trading the markets, reading books, and actually putting my own money learning from the markets. I have paid my dues and tuition to get this thick skin in the market.

Having said that, my risk tolerance is different depending on what I'm talking about. If you ask me if I'm risking everything that I have saved up for my next vacation or something else that's short term, I'd say no. But if you ask me about my long term funds, you can bet I'm in riskier assets.

With the Apple stock example, I might have scared you. Some of you might say, "I could never live through that kind of drop." Actually what's scarier are those that say, "I would never be stupid enough to buy Apple at 700." While that may be true, there were extremely intelligent fund managers out there with their CFA and MBAs that bought the stock at $700. What makes you think that you wouldn't have listened to these analysts of the street and join the hype when a lot of people were thinking the stock would go to $1,000?

On the flipside, I don't want you to think that stocks are risky. There are risky stocks and there are stocks that aren't. You need to think about businesses because you are essentially buying into a business when you buy a stock. Some businesses are riskier than others. Some businesses are seasonal while others are around year around. Some businesses are for only certain markets (think luxury goods and big margins) while other businesses sell products that everyone needs (think consumer staples and lower margins).

Use some common sense and don't worry about share prices. Think about the underlying business. You obviously don't want to buy a company at the top of its range unless you're trying to day trade a stock. This'll take me into another tangent, but there are trading systems that look for companies that have high a 52-week or all time high. It's a momentum trading system because they look to ride the momentum higher and hope it keeps going. A very viable trading system, but for the average investor it's too hard to decipher.

If you are looking to buy a solid company and you determine that to be McDonald's because while it's unhealthy, everyone needs (yes needs) McDonald's. Ok, maybe not everyone, but you get the point, there are a lot of people that just have to have McDonald's breakfast and I'm guilty of it too because I love their breakfast menu.

So if you are buying McDonald's, what is risk to you? What sort of risk are you willing to take? Are you able to hold it forever? When are you going to sell it? Where are you going to buy it? Why are you holding it? Is it for the dividend? Do you just like it because it's McDonald's? Do you know what the future holds for McDonald's? Are you expecting McDonald's to send you a quarterly Big Mac coupon? Do you simply like logo and nothing else?

These are just some of the numerous questions you could and should ask yourself. In fact you could compile a list for yourself for investment you make.

For every investment I make I have certain criteria that the investment has to meet. Some of those are things like, is it a solid company, does the stock price make sense? Where am I going to buy it? Where am I going to sell? What does the dividend yield look like? What are the various ratios looking like? P/E? P/B? Intrinsic value? No missed dividend payments? Consistent dividend growth? Where does all of this compare with the company's industry peers?

The more questions you have, the more comfortable you will be. Even with all that the company could fall the day after you buy the stock. You just don't know. That's how the markets are. But you want to be well equipped and be prepared mentally for anything since it's all about being prepared. That's what risk is about. Understanding how prepared you when all hell breaks loose.

When the financial crisis occurred in 2008, everyone panicked. There was good reason to be, it was a sharp, harsh, and ugly fall. People weren't prepared for it, and I don't blame them it's hard to prepare for something like that. But now that we have the experience behind us and even if you didn't have money involved, you should be aware that something like that can happen and will likely happen again. It might not happen to that extent or it could be a lot worse, but something will happen. History does not repeat itself, but history also has many brothers, sisters, cousins, great grandchildren that like to follow what history does. In one form or another, it will repeat itself.

If you spend enough time to prepare and understand your risk, you should be able to bare the pain. You'll feel your stomach turn, but as long as you don't hit the sell button and take huge losses when you should actually be buying, then you'll be fine. Where there is fear, there is opportunity. When everyone is panicking, that's when you need to be calmer than ever. Is there really a need to be panicking so much? Just a little something to think about.

Investing in the Stock Market and Understanding the Risks involved

We already talked about risk and what you need to watch out for. When people think risk, they usually think the stock market. Sure there are riskier things in the world, art investing, antique cars, precious metals, card collections, foreign exchange (forex), just to name a few. And for those that were wondering, gambling is not a type of investing!

The stock market isn't risky if you know what you're doing much like riding a bike isn't risky if you know how to ride one. What makes the stock market risky is that there are unknown factors that will uncover themselves at the worst of times and make the market or individual stock fall without warning. There are so many factors that could do this, natural disasters, local and global economic releases, industry news, new laws and regulations, company scandals, and much much more.

So how do you avoid all this? You can't. What you can do is diversify which means you buy different stocks so that you reduce the risk of your portfolio being affected by a one single factor. This is done by adding investments to your portfolio that aren't positively correlated which means they aren't too related to what each other does.

So if you buy stocks of a Canadian financial institution, US energy stock, and an English luxury brand, chances are you have lower portfolio risk in comparison to owning a bank in Canada and the US.

Within the stock market, there are different types of stocks. Aside from the different industries, there are company sizes. You've probably heard about small-cap stocks before. Well that means that company has a small market capitalization. Market capitalization is calculated by multiplying the number of outstanding shares by the current price per share. The actual size definition will depend on the market you're referring to. In the US a small cap company may actually be a mid-cap company in Canada just because the companies in the US are so much bigger.

So where am I going with all this? Well a smaller company naturally has more risk because they don't have economies of scale, a strong brand, a loyal customer base among other things. This means that a smaller company has to take bigger risks just to service never mind trying to get market share.

So if you flip this, the larger more mature companies have a strong chance of surviving and hence have less risk overall. Mature companies also usually pay a solid dividend that they increase regularly.

Now I want to pause here before I go further. Think about what I just said. If you buy a stock of a mature company that pays a dividend, chances are they will increase the dividend. If you buy a stock of such a company today for say $50 that pays a $0.50 quarterly dividend or $2.00 annually, then it's yielding 4% annually. That's not bad.

But if this same company increases their dividend annually and 10 years down the road the dividend is now $0.75 quarterly or $3.00 annually. Your cost base (the price you bought the stock at) obviously hasn't changed unless you bought more but that's beside the point I'm trying to make here. At $3.00 annually, the stock is now yielding 6%. That's not bad is it? If you made the right decision, chances are this stock will continue to increase their dividends over time.

I find this something that isn't talked too much. If you buy mutual funds, you unfortunately won't reap these benefits and maybe this is why because the big banks and all investment firms want you to buy their mutual fund.

I guess I would wrong if I said you didn't reap the benefits at all, it's just it would be hard to tell because mutual funds have way too many holdings for you to see the benefit directly. In addition, the mutual fund may sell the stock we are talking about prematurely and then buy it back again at a higher price. You will never know whereas if you were creating your own investment portfolio you will be able to see how every investment is done because you'll be placing all of the trades.

The stock market is only as risky as you make it. If you invest in stocks that carry have a higher volatility then yes your investment portfolio may incur unnecessary risk just because you bought those stocks. But if you buy mature stocks that still a solid chance of giving your capital appreciation while paying you nice dividends you aren't taking as much risk. Yes when the market as a whole falls, these stocks will fall too. But because these mature stocks are strong enough, most of them will recover and likely come out stronger as we've seen over the past few years.

The stock market can be risky, but it all comes down to the decisions you make. Much like when you drive your car. Who do you think has a higher chance of being in an accident? Someone driving at 50km/hr or 100km/hr?

The Power of an Automatic Contribution Plan

Chances are, when you visit your local branch you're heard a pitch from the bank teller about how important it is to stash money away every month or paycheck into an investment of some sort. As pesky and annoying as it is to hear this everytime you visit a bank branch (or lack thereof), it actually is very important for you to put money away on a consistent basis.

Someone once said, the key to successful investing is, "start early, keep doing it, and stay patient." That's it. Let's look at an example.

If you started investing today and put in $1,000 into your account and added just $25 a week for the same 10 years and at 6%, you would have $19,620.41. Not bad right?

The key here is to be disciplined and to make the investing painless. Most people can easily afford $25 a week. Trust me, if you work even part time in North America or any country with a decent wage, it's possible. By simply stashing this amount away, you have the potential to have a big amount saved for your future.

Just think of how much money you could save if you were to put more in, or put more money in as you get raises or get a better job! Isn't that an exciting thought? I'll give you another scenario.

If you invest $5,000 today and put in $100 a week at the same 10 year timeframe and 6% return, you would have $80,303.13. That's not too bad either.

In either case, we're only looking at a 10-year timeframe, which honestly isn't that long. If you're 20 years old and want to save for a downpayment, this is a great example of what can be accomplished over that 10 years.

We talked about figuring out your retirement number earlier in the book, in order to achieve that number you need to help yourself by making automatic contributions into an investment account on a regular basis and never cancel the contributions unless you're in an extreme situation. And having to go on a vacation is not an extreme situation.

Part 3: Everyday Life Best Practices

What One less Vanilla Latte a Week can mean for your finances!

Pretty much every single one of us has coffee breaks. It's a part of our daily routine and if you don't have that Tall Non-fat no foam half sweet vanilla latte with caramel drizzle at Starbucks at precisely 2:05pm everyday, your day just isn't complete. Some would probably go to the extent that without 2-3 coffee or lattes a day, they just won't be able to get through a tough day at work without physically harming someone.

Honestly, if you're one of these people you should put this book done and to talk to a Psychologist right now. Don't get me wrong, I love coffee to death, I have 2-3 cups a day but I can operate without it and so can you. To get back to the point of this book, let's take a look at what it means to have one less vanilla latte a day. Even with the economy at Starbucks and their inflation rates, I believe under my detailed reports that their most recent pricing on a tall vanilla latte sets you back around $5.

$5 per day may not seem like much to you but it actually can make a huge difference in the long term. So let's take a look at next test sample Travis. Travis thinks he's much better off than most since he only consumes through 3 Tall Vanilla Lattes per week. Good for him, in fact he could probably have more but he's really good at holding back on his urges for the sweet stuff, he just has more chocolate on his bad days.

Anyway, using a 7% return and saving the $5 every week, and stashing away that money away for the 30 years until

Travis' retirement, we would end up with $19,519.54! That's <u>one</u> less vanilla latte a week!

This just goes to show how much of a difference it makes to be saving those few dollars a week. You can of course implement the 50/50 rule here too. Every time that you don't buy that latte, give yourself $2 and put it in a piggy bank or an online savings account at your bank so that you can buy something for yourself. Resist the urge of having 25 lattes and you'll have enough money for a decent dinner for you and your date this weekend!

<u>Smoking Less Could Save More than your Life</u>

At 1 Pack a Day at $5 per pack with 5% annual interest for 25 years.
PMT = $25 N = 25 years * 52 = 1,300 weeks I/Y = 5%/52=0.09615 PV=0
FV = $64,694.43
I thought I'd make things more complicated by giving you what these steps look like on a financial calculator. If you're up for you it, you should spend the money to buy one. It's a pretty good investment and you'll be able to do all these calculations on your own.

You've heard it before, smoking isn't good for you. Now that's breaking news! Your friends and family have probably given you a million different reasons as to why you should stop smoking. One of the biggest reasons to quit smoking is for your health. Lung cancer isn't the only risk you have to worry about, smoking can lead to numerous illnesses that can shorten your life significantly. But I'm not writing about health, I'm writing about saving money and I'll give you 64,694 reasons why you should stop smoking.

If you smoke a pack a day and spend a very modest $5 a pack a day, live in an environment where you can earn 5% (we'll talk more about this in a bit) and smoke for 25 years, you can save a whopping $64,694.43 over that span of time. Sounds insane doesn't? That's a lot of money that could have been used to make you a much happier person, sometimes it just takes someone to slap you in the face with reality to give you some motivation to quit.

Breaking the Ugly Habit

So I've given you a reality check but what can you do? Everyone knows it general it's very hard to quit. Smoking is an addiction that is extremely hard to break. I know friends that have tried only to go back smoking a day, week, or month later because they can't resist the temptation.

Here's one tip that you can use to motivate yourself to stop smoking. Get a piggy bank or something of that nature to store cash. Everytime you don't smoke, reward yourself. There's 20 cigarettes in a pack and if a box costs $5, so that translates to roughly 25 cents per cigarette. Everyday that you don't smoke, deposit $5 into the piggy bank and keep doing this much like with the vanilla latte. Empty the piggy bank at the end of the month and deposit these funds into a dedicated bank account or better yet invest the funds and watch your savings grow.

The best way to make this rewarding is to separate what you save.

Bad Breath isn't good for your Social Status Either

Heavy smokers are just plain old nasty. Ever had a conversation and while talking to them get a whiff of their horrible smoker breath? I sure have and it's disgusting, why would you want to add insult to injury (to yourself) by having such horrible breath. I don't care how attractive you are, having bad breath (gum can only go so far), is a hugely unappealing.

Save on Banking and Credit Card Fees

When was the last time you spent time looking at how much money you're spending on banking fees and credit card annual fees? I know of a lot of people that mindlessly sign up for bank accounts with services they don't need and spend $10-15 a month without even thinking about it. If you need the extra services like bank drafts, overdraft protection, etc. it might make sense to spend that extra amount but if you aren't then you're essentially wasting $180 a year. Over 30 years, that's nearly $12,500 you could have saved with 5% interest!

Analyzing your Banking Usage
So how can you save money on banking fees? First you need to analyze what services you need at the bank. Banking goes way beyond deposits, withdrawals, and bill payments. If that's all you do, you need the basic account and you'll be able to get this for free most of the time. Some banks don't require a minimum balances while others will. Some banks might want you to have certain

products such as an investment and credit card to get a free banking account which is ok too since if you're reading this book, you should be using your credit and saving your money through an investment.

If you need other services like an overdraft protection, free checks, unlimited transactions, and others, you might consider spending money on banking fees as this may save you money in the long terms. Spend some time on your bank's website to see what you really need and the next time you're in the bank have your account package changed. You might even be able to change your account package online, it depends on your bank.

If you do need certain services, instead of going for banking packages, it could be cheaper simply getting those certain services on the side, if the bank offers them outside of banking packages. Overdraft protection is a classic example. Overdraft protection basically covers you in case you put your account balance in negative but still need payments and cheques to go through without balancing. The banks will usually provide this service for a few dollars per month.

Shop around! I've heard many say Credit Unions have cheap bank accounts while other banks may be offering a cheaper account to suit your needs. The thing about credit unions is that they're usually smaller and therefore have less ATMs when you need them. It all depends on your needs so do a little analysis, it's the best way to ensure you'll be happy with what you get. Just because something is cheaper it doesn't necessarily mean it's better.

Decide on the Right Credit Card

A lot of people shun credit card fees without looking into the details. Credit cards that have annual fees, have them for a reason and it usually means more benefits and perks by paying that fee. The perk could be better point conversion, insurance, and more. If you travel a lot, some cards have travel insurance attached to them if you purchase the vacation through your card. Others have great point conversions that could lead to great rewards. Just be sure you know what you're working towards. I have talked to many people that have a ridiculous amount of points saved up with no idea how to use them. Some credit cards offer cash rewards as well, while this might not be the best bang for the buck, it's better than putting your points to waste.

If you use your debit card a lot and as a result are paying higher banking fees, I hope by reading this you will change. Using your credit card is so much better and safer, as long as you can control your spending. Your credit card purchases are usually covered by your credit card company giving you that extra peace of mind in case something happens. It'll depend on your credit card as to how far this insurance will go.

Another huge advantage of credit cards over debit cards is that you have unlimited transactions. Credit cards make money every time you use their card so they want you to use their cards so it wouldn't make sense for them to charge you per transaction, they charge the merchant (the person you're paying) instead. By having unlimited transactions, you have no reason to be using your debit card. This should eliminate your need of unlimited transactions through your banking account. Why use your debit card for everyday purchases when you could be racking up points on your credit card?

Save First Buy Later or Never

In the old days, everything was bought with cash. There was no credit card, this meant that you had to save your money to buy something before you could actually get it. Today, the world is reversed. You can buy a lot of things with no money down and simply use your credit card or your line of credit with your bank. That's why so many people are in debt and are having trouble getting out of debt because they can't seem to resist the lure of credit.

In order to become financially intelligent and responsible, you have to go back to the old days and actually save the money before you buy something. Obviously, for some items it's financially intelligent to take on the debt and buy the item first and pay it down. Read the chapter on Smart Debt vs. Stupid Debt later on in this book and you'll understand what the difference is. For the purposes of this chapter, I'm talking about items that fall into the Stupid debt category that are items that aren't necessities. Items that you want to make your life more enjoyable, also known as luxury items.

So let's say for example that you're looking to buy a brand new pair of shoes that costs $500. Most people will go straight to the store, and tell themselves that they're only looking and they won't buy the shoes. Of course, when they go to Nine West or Nordstrom they find those beautiful Manolo's that are actually on sale for only $600. These shoes retail at $800 so you're actually saving $200!

Even though it's $100 over your budget it's no big deal because you're "saving" so much money and these shoes will gone before you know it and they never go on sale! Out comes the credit card and you make the purchase. You now are the proud owner of a beautiful pair of pink Manolo's and have increased your stupid debt by $600. Don't you just love how people justify the purchases in their minds? Don't lie, I know you've done it before too. So have I. There's a reason why I have 6 guitars.

Sure you might not spend $600 on Manolo's but you might spend $100, $200 or $1,000. The figure does matter but what matters more is the mindset behind your purchases. If you don't pay off your credit card the same month you're paying around 20% annual interest on your entire credit card balance (including everything else besides the Manolo's) until you cough up the funds to pay for it.

What you should be doing is saving money every time you get a paycheck or have some sort of inflow in cash. Create a bank account named "Big Purchase Fund" like we talked about earlier. Your fixed expenses like rent, groceries, transportation costs, and hydro should take priority. With the extra funds you have from your paycheck, you should divide that among your savings for the future and savings for yourself. The Big Purchase fund account will be savings for you.

It's a pretty simple concept that takes discipline. Let's say you decide to save $50 per paycheck and that you get paid every 2 weeks. So in order to get $600 saved, ignoring any interest, it will take you 6 months to get the $600 you need to buy those shoes. The great thing about this is because you've waited so long you might not want those shoes anymore and could want something else that costs less. Now you have money saved for something else.

I also like to have an idea as to what's next on my list of things to buy for the Big Purchase fund. I keep a spreadsheet of all the items I want to buy and work towards those goals. It's gratifying when you reach a goal and are actually able to buy that item. This is usually the fund with the highest balance that I carry because most items on my Big Purchase fund are at least a couple hundred dollars.

Understanding Your Current Lifestyle

I know I've been telling you to look over your monthly expenses and budget constantly but when was the last time you really took a look at your spending habits? It's one thing to take a look and analyze your monthly expenses but it's another to actually take action. In North America, we're prone to taking on a lot of debt. Unfortunately, the average person in Canada and the US rack up more debt than they save. That means most people make purchases with their credit card or line of credit and keep that balance sitting there.

That isn't healthy for your finances and just because everyone around you is doing something doesn't mean you should be too. So you need to understand and really take a look at your current lifestyle. If you live in a big city, this is very important because your friends and people in general around you will be spending a lot of money. Just paying rent and eating is expensive enough, but when you start to factor in the money you spend when you're out and about, the need to look good in decent clothing, and having that BMW M3 can get very costly.

We have our wants and our needs. Our wants are the luxuries in life, things that you can do without when push comes to shove. Our needs are the necessities. When you analyze your monthly expenses, split up what you have to pay for (rent, groceries, insurance, hydro, etc.) from the things you don't really need to pay for (daily coffee, eating out, car payment, cable, etc.) and look at how much you are spending in the latter category. Trust me, you'll be quite surprised as to how much you're spending.

I do this with clients quite often. I go through their monthly budget and look at everything and they don't really realize how much they're spending until someone digs deep and asks them to spill it all out. This is what you need to do, analyze it and don't be embarrassed about it.

I'm not asking you to be cheap. I'm asking you to be frugal and to reward yourself as you go. You can still go on your extravagant vacations or buy that new car, but plan for it. Don't make it an impulse purchase because you'll regret it later. I've heard before that if you're making a big purchase and I mean very big like a car, you should let it sit for 30 days and come back to that decision. If you still think it makes sense, then go for it. But you better have saved enough for it, and if you're going to have monthly payments then you better have factored that into your monthly budget.

Really, spend some time and analyze your current lifestyle. A tweak here and there can make a big difference and will actually allow you to have a better lifestyle (possibly more expensive) down the road. Remember, planning it all out is the key.

Part 4: Dealing with Debt

<u>Don't cut up your Credit Cards!</u>

I'm intrigued by the number of financial "gurus" out there that tell people to cut up their credit cards and use cash for every purchase they make. Sure you might be in debt to the point that you've maxed out your credit cards. But at that point, you can't use your credit card anyway and by cutting them up, you're only admitting defeat. You're not dealing with the problem, you're only avoiding it and unless you get to the root of the problem, you're going to end up repeating your mistakes again once you pay down your debt.

Take a close look at what the issues are. Sure, that wallet-sized plastic makes it easy to buy almost anything you want. But, what's the real problem? Is it the credit card or is it you? If you answered the credit card, you really need to get someone to smack you back into reality. Credit cards are a great tool to build your credit and financial discipline. If you can learn to use credit cards properly, you'll actually be better off than most individuals that make much more money than you do.

If you want to achieve financial freedom in life, you need to understand how to deal with credit face on. Sure you could live in the primitive age and stick to the cash-only mindset, but you're actually wasting a lot of money and convenience by doing so. Any decent credit card out there has either a point accumulation benefit or a cash back system. Some card will pay you back 2% for your purchases on things like groceries and gas a 1% on everything else. That adds up to a pretty nice benefit on your daily purchases.

If you go the point route, then you need to do a little math and figure out what point rewards yield the best dollar per point yield. Some rewards might seem like a good deal but they often aren't and I've found that some travel rewards are the best deals. You need to be careful of blackout periods for some cards as there might only be one or two seats on flights available for everyone that uses that reward system. However, by using your credit card, you just might pay for your next vacation. Simply by using your credit card on your daily necessity purchases, you could save hundreds or even thousands of dollars.

Using a credit card can help you more than by just getting cash back or accumulating points. If you pay your credit card balance in full every month, you won't have to pay a single penny in interest. Sure the credit card companies might not like you but at the end of the day, they still make money because every time you used your credit card, they take a percentage of the purchase price from the person that you made a purchase from.

By paying your entire balance in full every month, you are building credit history. The better your credit rating, the easier it will be to borrow money in the future and the better the interest rate that you will get. A lower interest rate will save you a huge amount of money in the longer term.

By making it so that you're on top of your credit card payments, not only are you helping your financial well being, you're also working on your financial discipline. If you keep track of your purchases and pay them back on time, you know that you have that obligation that it needs to be paid within 30 days or whenever your payment is due. Don't become like most credit card users and think that you can pay it off eventually. This is the sucker game that credit card companies want you to think, that's why they'll often send you letters of phone you telling you that you can increase the limit on your credit. There's no need for a high credit card limit. I usually use 10% of my credit card limit because that's all I need.

Smart Debt vs. Stupid Debt

When you borrow money, most people view it as a bad thing. At the end of the day you're borrowing someone else's money and have to pay interest on it until you pay off the debt in its entirety. It seems like you're only making the other party richer right? This can be true, but it really depends on what you borrow the money for.

Savvy individuals see debt as leverage, meaning they're using the money they borrow to increase their wealth. The rich do this all the time and probably have a lot more debt than the general public can imagine because most regular people think that the rich people just have a lot of cash lying around and bathe in $100 bills. Not to burst your bubble, but this isn't true.

Stupid debt is very simple. If you don't need it and it isn't going to bring you extra income, it's stupid debt. This sort of debt will only dig a deeper whole for those that are already in debt and will slow down wealth accumulation for those that are trying to build their retirement fund or are trying to save for something meaningful. If you're buying shoes on your credit card and paying a portion of it off monthly, this is stupid debt. If you're buying a car that is beyond your means and borrowing money to pay it off, this is stupid debt. Having said that, if you're buying a car and you absolutely need and it's well within your means, this isn't stupid debt, it's a necessity. See where I'm going?

So what exactly is smart debt? It does seem counterintuitive at first but it really isn't. The easy answer is that smart debt can lead to better financial well-being either in the immediate future or eventually. It all depends on how much risk you are willing to take. For some, it is buying a home and getting a mortgage. Some financial "gurus" think that buying a house and having a mortgage is stupid debt, but it really isn't for the most part.

You often hear the term "house rich, cash poor." That's when the buyer is putting so much money into the house that they are left with little cash and are often putting a large portion of the their income paying the mortgage, maintenance, and other costs associated with having their own home. So is this stupid debt? Not necessarily, sure they're stranded for cash, but they made an investment that will help them in the future. In the long run, if they pay off their mortgage, they won't have to worry about paying rent or mortgage for one of the necessities in life.

It's the purpose behind the spending that is important. And the key question here is, "is it within your means?" Whether if it's a home, car or anything else you have to do the math and figure out what you can afford. I've made decisions in life that had my back against the wall in terms of cash flow, but I stuck to it because I knew it was within my means and I knew I was making a smart debt decision. Something to consider is depending on where you live in the world, housing prices are so high that you have to go outside of your comfort zone in order to be able to buy and that's a factor that goes into the equation of home buying.

Another form of smart debt is taking on extra debt to create a new source of income. This can be money that you borrow to buy investments of any kind. It could stocks, real estate, fixed income investments and more. The problem here is that you need to really understand what you are getting into and be willing to take on risk. Investing is beyond the scope of this book, but if you want to take on smart debt and frankly want to become financially free eventually, you need to know how to invest and take on risk.

The more comfortable you become at taking on more smart debt and the less stupid debt you have, the closer to financial freedom you will become. It's very simple yet very difficult for many people to do this. This difference alone will make or break how successful you will be in life. It all comes down to being able to deal with your temptations and focusing on building wealth, that's what smart debt is all about.

Unfortunately, you can only choose one. If you have a lot of stupid debt, it'll be very hard to have smart debt. On the other hand, if you have a lot of smart debt, you might not need to take on any stupid debt at all because if you do things right, you might not need to borrow any money to buy the luxuries you want to buy.

<u>Pay Down Your Mortgage Faster</u>

In general, when you borrow money, you pay a higher interest rate than you would when you invest your money in safer investments such as term deposits or government bonds. This is because banks like their spread, in other words this is how the financial institutions make money on the money that they borrow from the government and other savers like you and recycle that money to lend to others.

So when you've gotten a new stream of cash whether if it's from an increase in pay or if it's from an inheritance, the first thing that should come to mind is where do I put this money for the best return on investment. If your first thought was, "what can I buy with this money?" You fail the test of financial discipline and should get your significant other to spank you a few times.

Getting back to the point, while it depends on the interest rate environment, it is often a very good investment to pay down your mortgage faster because you will be saving on interest not only in the short term but in the long term. This is because when you make extra payments you're your mortgage, you're eating directly into the principal of the mortgage.

Having a mortgage means you have the power of compounding working against you, therefore if you pay it down you save yourself at least partially from this compounding effect.

Now you're probably saying, but I've got a fixed and closed mortgage, how do you expect me to pay down my mortgage faster? Let's define what those mortgage terms mean that you always read about in the newspaper.

Let's say you have a 5.0% 5 Year Fixed Closed Mortgage with a 25 year Amortization. This means that you have a 5.0% interest rate that is fixed (cannot be changed) for the 5-year term that you have agreed upon with your bank or broker. A closed mortgage means that you cannot payout your mortgage earlier. You might be able to but not without a heft penalty. Sometimes it makes sense to pay the penalty when interest rates have fallen significantly, you have to do the math for this to see if it really makes sense, but that's not what I'm trying to get at here.

Finally, a 25-year amortization means that this is the amount of time that it will take you to completely payoff your mortgage. To clarify, when the currently 5-year term of your mortgage is up, you will need to re-finance with your bank or broker (you should shop around) to get the best rate at the time.

So now we have the definitions out of the way, you need to look at the fine print of your mortgage. Most banks nowadays allow extra payments and annual payments straight to the principal. Extra payments usually mean you can pay a minimum amount up to the actual mortgage payment at the time of your mortgage payment. This extra amount that you pay will go directly to your mortgage principal, immediately reducing the interest you will pay on the remaining amount of your mortgage because you a smaller amount outstanding than you would if you didn't pay this amount.

An annual payment is usually a lump sum that you are allowed to pay against your mortgage principal. I've seen this go to around 10% of the outstanding mortgage principal. If you have any cash lying around (and you should if you've been reading and implementing this book), then you should put at least a part of those funds against your mortgage. It even makes sense to use part of your retirement funds to pay down your mortgage because it is often very hard to get a return like you would paying down your mortgage in the markets, especially if you are a risk averse (you hate risk) investor.

The one thing about annual payments is that you're only allowed one payment. So if you make a 1% payment and want to pay more, you usually aren't allowed at all or have to pay a penalty. So plan these things out before you pay some random amount. Another thing to note is that there is a window of time that you will be able to pay this amount and it's usually within a month of the anniversary date of the mortgage.

A lot to think about but it's actually really simple. If you have extra cash then use it to pay down your mortgage. Paying down debt isn't exactly the most exciting thing to do, but it can significantly help you in the long term.

Let's look at an example. Let's say we were using the mortgage terms we had earlier and that it was a $400,000 mortgage at 5% - 5 year fixed and closed with a 25-year amortization. Just by making one extra double-up payment a year you would be able to pay off your mortgage in its entirety by 3.6 years faster! In addition, in the 21.4 years it will take you to pay off your mortgage you will save $49,101.51 in interest. Now, if that doesn't sound like a good deal, I don't know what is.

The same can be said for an anniversary payment towards your mortgage. You don't need to maximize your payments, just put whatever you have against the mortgage and it will make a huge difference in the long term.

One more factor to consider when determining your mortgage payments is the payment frequency of your mortgage. Instead of paying your mortgage on a monthly basis, try to pay it on a bi-weekly basis. The only difference here is the frequency of your payments. If it's monthly you pay 12 times a year. If it's bi-weekly you pay every 2 weeks so your pay 26 times a year. The actual total amount you pay throughout the year is the exact same for both payment frequencies. It just takes some financial discipline on your part to ensure that you have the funds in your bank account that you will be able to pay the mortgage.

So what's the difference? Well, just by changing the frequency you will save $3,835.39 over the course of the mortgage term. Sure it isn't as eye popping as the double-up payments, but this is without paying an extra cent towards your mortgage! If you increase the frequency to weekly then you save roughly an extra $550 or so. Not bad right?

People are very passive with mortgages because they don't understand what it is. They just think that the lowest interest rates are the best and they don't look at the fine print. Sometimes a higher interest rate with better clauses is a better deal in the end. Sometimes it isn't, it depends on what you're looking for. Either way, you should be looking to pay down your mortgage when you can. Don't think rates are everything because they aren't.

In the case you are stuck with a mortgage that doesn't allow double-up payments or anniversary payments, what you can do is save money until it is time to refinance your mortgage. When that time comes, you can pay down your mortgage and refinance that lower amount with your financial institution. So say you had $335,000 outstanding when your mortgage is up for renewal, if you have $15,000 sitting in your investment account doing nothing, use those funds and renew your mortgage at $320,000.

A house is usually the biggest investment we all make so don't be passive with how you deal with. Get rid of the mortgage as soon as you can and put that money to better use such as creating passive income streams so that you can retire earlier. That should be your goal. Not having a mortgage is absolutely huge.

The Best Guaranteed Investment with the Lowest Risk, Get Out of Debt First!

Many of us look for the best investments while reducing our risk and we often forget that we have a guaranteed investment right in front of our eyes. Yes, paying down your debt is often the best investment you can get because there's no risk involved and it usually means getting a better return than most investments out there. This works just like paying down your mortgage, but better.

If you are carrying credit card debt, this is a no-brainer since it means you are paying 20% or more in annual interest. If you have credit cards from places like Home Depot or Walmart, interest rates are often significantly higher. Don't think that you're outsmarting yourself by having a low-interest credit card which has "only 12%", who are you kidding? What investment can you get that pays you a 12% return? Don't forget that you are paying 12% interest with after-tax dollars, which means you have to earn much more than this to actually pay that 12%.

Let's go down the debt food chain and look at lines of credit, which often have lower interest rates. This usually depends on the relationship you have with your bank and could be as low as 6-7% if you have a good credit rating or if it's a secured line of credit. Line of credit rates vary hugely depending on where you live, your bank, and your credit. The average norm for non-secured lines of credit seems to be 7-10%. Having a secured line of credit simply means that you put up collateral towards your loan. The most common one is where you use your home as collateral and get a big portion of the equity in your home available for your usage with a low interest rate.

This is where the dumb and smart are separated. The dumb will say, "great! I have extra cash at my disposal! Let's go spend some of it on stupid things!" Once they get access to this extra "cash" in the line of credit, they'll look to buy clothes, eat out more often and put themselves more and more in debt.

On the other hand, smart people will look at this extra resource as an extra backup plan and look to pay down all of their outstanding debt that carries extra interest, like car loans and credit card balances. After all of their high interest debt is paid off, they will focus on paying down the lowest interest rate debt last.

If you have a mountain of debt, you could consider getting a consolidation loan so that you can pay off all of your debt and have a new loan, which has a new interest rate (which should be lower than your previous debt) and focus on paying off one debt. Sometimes paying off debt is psychological, and by only having one to focus on could help you pay it off. Whatever it takes, make sure your debt does not get out of hand. That's why it's so important to budget your spending so that you don't put too much on your credit card or buy a car that you just simply can't afford.

But if you've already made stupid decisions and as we all know, we can't turn back time, you have to do what it takes to get yourself out of this mess. Chip away at it in pieces. In all honesty, you should be putting any excess cash against your debts and that's what most financial gurus will tell you. I think this is important, but I personally don't want to completely sacrifice my happiness to pay off debt while feeling miserable. Reward yourself along the way so that you know you're doing a good thing while have some fun doing it!

Part 5: Tying it all Together

Discipline

Discipline is an attribute you need to be successful in anything you do in life. Without it, you will be an average person that procrastinates and throws out goals and dreams as if it were a normal thing. But with discipline, you give yourself a strong chance of succeeding in any venture you take on.

Discipline with your finances is no different. Every time you buy something unnecessary or go on an unplanned extravagant vacation, the more you eat into your financial discipline. You procrastinate and hold off thinking that eventually you'll find the time and discipline to save money and invest for your financial future. Your freedom. Unfortunately, what many people fail to realize is that you can't reach your financial goals overnight unless you win the lottery. And trust me, winning the lottery is not a sound financial plan. Although some people sadly bank on it.

So how do you develop discipline if you don't have it? It isn't easy, even for the most discipline people. You have to build it slowly and you have to keep it in check because if you don't, you'll easily become undisciplined.

I've said this time and time again; you have to create a plan. Have short, midterm, and long-term goals. Make the long-term goals things like retirement, paying off your mortgage. Your short and midterm goals should be more achievable in their respective time frames. Short term should be within 1 year and you should reward yourself every time you hit a short term goal to entice yourself to work hard to stick with the plan and achieve your goal.

We all like rewards so this is a great way to develop discipline.

The obvious thing to note is not to overdo the reward for the goal achieved. Just because you managed to save $1,000 and stash it away in an invested, doesn't mean you can "reward" yourself by going on a $5,000 vacation. That's not how it works. A more suitable reward would be going for a movie night or a dinner to celebrate, within reason of course!

Be Generous when it counts

One of my personal goals in life is to become a philanthropist. I know it's not something I should openly talk about because it's something that you just do and not really expect any recognition for it. And that's the plan. But I bring it up here because once you become wealthy, I want you to think the same way. I obviously can't impose this on you, but I want you to understand how a little bit for you can go a very long way for others.

We all have different values, cultures, common sense, wants and needs. But regardless of your nationality or culture, $50 you donate to help a good cause is $50 that could save someone's life. Spend some time to really think about that. It's a good feeling to make a difference in someone's life.

The money or time that you donate could mean a source of water or food for a person, family, or town. It could put children through education or get them out of poverty. And it could save lives in a variety of different ways such as providing basic medical care for those in need or providing basic shelter.

The tough part sometimes is where you donate the money and time. Some of these charitable organizations that are supposed to be non-profit have the people that lead them living extravagant lifestyles, which makes you scratch your head. It sure makes me scratch mine. But, there are people out there that really want to help and really want to make a difference.

There's no pressure. And I don't want you doing this with your life savings. But it would be nice if you could set aside a small budget from your monthly budget or put something in your will (you do have one right?) to help out your favorite charitable organization.

Understanding who you are and what your life goals are

We're all busy, very busy. We know we need to treasure our lives, each and every day of it. But the problem with the vast majority is that we take most things in life for granted. We take for granted everything from our work, our friends, our loved ones, our lifestyle, and much more. When you lose it, you understand how big of impact each one had on your life, yet until you lose it you never realize it. Even if you think you do, you don't. Even if your best friend loses one of these things, you think you understand their pain, but in reality you most likely don't.

What's worse is that we go beyond taking our surroundings for granted and we get greedy. We want more. If you live in a nice house, you want a bigger and better house. If you drive a nice car, you want to update it regularly and get a nicer car. Chances are it isn't your fault, it's the society you live in. If you live in a small town this might not be the case and if you honestly don't care about any of this, then kudos to you. You've already found the secret to early financial freedom. But for most people, how they look in the grand social status scheme of things is more important than how they are doing financially.

Where am I trying to get with all this? You need to sit down with yourself and spend some time figuring out what your values are. What is important to you? Forget the social norms or what is expected of people. Forget what "they" say. You are you, and that's all that matters.

So what is it in life that keeps you going? Whatever that might be, however twisted it may or may not be, this is what you should treasure in life. Write it all down, write whatever you need to write down. I'm not going to give you a secret formula because there's no such thing. We all think differently draw maps, webs, make a list, the important thing is that you write it down and think about the elements of your life that make you happy.

Happiness doesn't come cheap. And I'm not talking about money. Money is only a small part of the huge equation. To attain happiness we need to know the other half of it, the pain, stress and agony of our lives. Only by knowing these horrible things do we understand what true happiness is. Why do you think Eric Clapton was able to write such wonderful songs? Because he experienced and endured living agony. I've personally learned lessons in life that I'll never forget, and while I feel and hope that it has made me a better person, it's the pain and agony that made me learn those lessons.

Achieving financial freedom isn't hard. The media and financial institutions want you to think it's near impossible because the media is paid the big bucks by those financial institutions so that you walk into one of their branches to get your money to invest with them. Don't get me wrong, this isn't a bad thing at all. If you're going to invest at all, you should invest your money with people you can actually trust and can have a long-term relationship with.

We all have a lot of things going on in life. We get distracted easily and before you know it, years have passed. Don't you always think to yourself how quickly time passes? If that's the case, then you need to take control and get time to be on your side. With a proper financial plan, you give yourself a chance to make this happen.

Keep it Simple!

If you're like me, you'll spend countless hours reading books on financial planning and investments, you'll most likely spend a ton of time reading investment blogs, doing detailed fundamental and technical analysis of all sorts of companies and, you'll even go as far as talking about investing in your sleep! You're probably rolling your eyes, and I hope you are because you definitely don't want to be like me, well for the most part. It's good to be hungry for knowledge but just like with anything do it in moderation.

So as I have said, I have spent a lot of time studying all this stuff. I've taken courses in Investing, Financial Planning, Accounting, Real Estate Appraisal, Commercial Real Estate, on this is on top of having an Honors University Degree at one of the top Universities in the world. How's that for credibility? I also have an Investment designation among other things but I'll stop the bragging and get to my point.

The more I learn, study, and research the more it all gets confusing. The reason for this is because with all sorts of opinions, information, and argument, it can get pretty messy in your head after a while. What's rational for one person may be irrational for another. Going back to risk, what you think is risky might not seem risky at all for me.

Let's take technical analysis for example. I've studied different charts, chart patterns, oscillators, indicators for countless hours. I have spent time backtesting, looking at different timeframes, and actually traded real money on all of this. And guess what I have read a ridiculous amount of material about all this as well. So after all this research and reading, you're probably thinking that when I look at the screen for any particular stock or investment, I must have this crazy map with a million lines that's supposed to quote some sort of investment right? Wrong!

Because of all of the mumble jumble I've read, I've learned that one you need to find what works for you, and two keep it as simple as you possibly can. Whoever said that simple is best is absolutely right. The simpler it is, the easier it is.

Unless, you want to make an appearance on CNBC and talk about this amazing technical trading system that uses a complicated algorithm with 14 indicators, 8 trend lines, and 12 oscillators and have the audience shut the TV off on you, keep it simple.

With your own financial planning, you want to keep it simple. Create a plan, write down the goals you want, write down how much risk you're willing to take, how you're going to do the investing, how long it's going to take, and what you're going to do when you reach those goals. You can add more but that's the jist of it, pretty simple yes?

That doesn't mean you should just sit on your butt, read my book and think that you're set for life. I mean, I'd be honored if you thought that, but the reality is my one book isn't going to suffice. For you to really appreciate this book, you'll need to spend time learning more. I can say that from experience. I read books like the *Intelligent Investor* when I was starting out and I didn't have the slightest clue what the book was talking about, but at this point I can almost fully appreciate what's written in that book, just to give one example.

The point is that just because I'm telling you to keep it simple doesn't mean to not read and learn. It means keep learning but keep the plan that you create as simple as you possibly can. We're all human, the more complicated the task at hand is the more we tend to procrastinate. But with financial planning and investing you just can't procrastinate or shy away from it. You have to face it head on and make it the best you.

The Life Long Goal of Financial Freedom

So, I think you've figured out that the goal of this book is to help you reach financial freedom. Stop and think about what that means. There's a reason why this book isn't title "How to become a millionaire/billionaire" or "The secret recipe to earn a Million dollars per hour." I'm not here to give you false hopes or to claim things that work when they really don't. That's not my goal at all. My goal is to help you simply this whole process and to realize that it really isn't all that complicated.

You don't need to have an investment or financial planning designation to learn how to manage your money and to be successful. If you spend time to understand what I've written in this book, you've earned the right to have the key to open the door to financial freedom. It's in every single one of you, it's just simply asking if you really want it.

Now, before I start sounding like a motivational speaker, which I really am not, let's look at what this book really does. It lays down the facts about what small amounts, invested over a long period can give you. In an earlier chapter I talked about how Rick needed to save $820 at a 7% return for 30 years to hit the $1,000,000 mark. You might think that 7% is ridiculous and it might be if you can't stomach any risk, but if you're an intelligent investor, it's possible to do consistently averaged out.

More than the return, I want you to focus on what that all means. I've done many different calculations in this book to hopefully hit the point home. Investing small regular amounts is the key to financial freedom. If you plan it right, you won't even need to deplete any of your investment portfolio ever!

Now what does financial freedom really mean? It means that you can wake up everyday, not go to work and still be able to live comfortably financially. Your passive income is in excess of all of your expenses combined. Isn't that a wonderful thought?

That's another reason why you need to dissect your monthly expenses. The better you control your monthly expenses the easier it will be for you to reach financial freedom. There's actually two parts to this.

First, if you reduce your monthly expenses and are a disciplined person, you'll be able to stash more money away into your investments with the money you save. This is key. If you save money but spend money elsewhere it defeats the purpose. Even if you put your money into investments like money market funds or GICs, it's better than spending it but you're still not going to get far just because the returns will be dismal. You must learn to take some risk in your investment portfolio. I'm not saying you have to own all stocks. I'm saying that you need to learn to have a portion of your investment portfolio in stocks, even if that's 20-30%. That 20-30% can make the different of you retiring 5-10 years early.

Second, the lower your monthly expenses, the easier it will be to reach financial freedom. This is because you need your investment portfolio to earn less than you would if your monthly expenses were higher. In the case of Rick, he needed $50,000 pre-tax income in order to support his lifestyle. After 30% tax, let's say that $50,000 is $35,000 or about $2917 a month. Now I don't know about you but that's a pretty big amount. For the vast majority of the people, that's more than enough to survive on.

But let's say you're able to live off of $2,500 a month including all of your expenses. This is where having that mortgage paid off helps too. Now all of sudden you're likely in a lower tax bracket which makes it that much easier to reach financial freedom. So let's say your average tax rate is now 25% instead of the 30%. That means you only need $42,858 a year to support your lifestyle. So by reducing your monthly budget by $417 a month, you reduce the pre-tax income that you need by $7,142! To help you with that calculation and confuse you more $417 x 12 months = $5004. It just goes to show what taxes can do to you and why tax planning and tax efficient returns are so important.

So now we need to look at the number $42,858. I can tell you in case it isn't obvious enough, $42,858 is a lot easier to tackle compared to $50,000. If you were to have the same 5% return as Rick's post-retirement portfolio, then you would need $857,160 in your investment portfolio. That's $142,840 less than the $1,000,000 of Rick's investment portfolio. Do you see how big of a difference it can make to be a little frugal, live in a cheaper area of the world, take one less vacation in a year, etc.?

I'll take this calculation further to show you what it takes for you to reach this number. We'll use the same numbers as with Rick. If you had 30 years with a 7% return, you would need to stash away $702.61 per month. That's about $108 less than with Rick's scenario.

Now this should tell you two things. The first is that you don't have to kill yourself to reach financial freedom. $700 isn't a small number but if you work hard enough, it isn't an impossible number to deal with either. It's the amount many people pay for their car loan payment. If it is for you, then I ask you a very simple question, do you need that car? With all these wonderful transportation options including ride share nowadays, I even question myself if I need a car.

The second thing this should tell you is that by only adding an extra $108 a month, you'll be able to hit that magic million dollar number. Isn't that kinda nice? Instead of saying that you have a "6 digit" investment portfolio, you can brag that you have a "7 digit" investment portfolio. Now, that'll turn heads at your next cocktail party.

There are a variety of factors that you do need to consider of course. You might not get the 7% return every year. But in reality, while you may have years where you might have a negative return or years with 3 or 4% returns but you'll also have years with 10 and 15% returns that will likely offset and possibly accelerate the growth of your investment portfolio.

You also need to realize that you don't need to be on the 30 year plan, you will have to invest more but you can shrink these numbers to 20, 15, 10 years and possibly shorter if you can afford to stash that much money away. So getting that second part time job or starting some on the side might seem a lot more enticing now that I have laid this out there.

As much as the large financial institutions or brokers want you to think how hard it is to become financially free, it really isn't. If you can live on a $1,500 or $2,000 monthly budget it hastens your plan to freedom.

Another factor you should look at are the fees involved with your investments. If you are putting your money in mutual funds make sure that you are getting the funds with the lowest fees. Smaller brokerage firms will have higher fees and will be sneaky and hit you with hidden fees like deferred sales charges, or will charge you a front-load fee which means you pay them for the privilege of being able to invest with them.

Why should you pay in order to have them make money? Always go for no-load mutual funds with lower MER (Management Expense Ratios). The bigger institutions usually have a lower MER so visit your local big bank, I hope you're dealing with one! Trust me, having worked at a major bank as much hate as they get it makes sense to bank with one. Sure the small players will have less or no fees, but no fees doesn't necessarily mean you're going to be better off. Don't be cheap, be smart!

I hope I was able to get you to understand how becoming financially free isn't as complicated as you might have heard it was. It sure isn't easy and will take time, but it sure isn't impossible. I hope I was I able to help you get one step closer to this amazing goal and dream. Trust me, it'll be worth it.

<u>Closing Notes</u>

I hope by reading this book you were able to learn something about planning for your financial freedom. I also hope I was able to take away some stress of this big daunting task. Dealing with money and personal finance is extremely stressful. That's why it's so important to simply everything as much as you can and worry about other important things in life like family, friends and making your life as fulfilling as possible. We only get one chance at this, so make it worthwhile.

If you read this book and still think financial planning and investing isn't for you, that's fine! I commend you for reading this book and at least trying. If this stuff bores you to death then that's fine, I'm sure you have other hobbies and things that interest you. There's no need you to force this stuff down your throat. Leave it to the professionals that are extremely passionate about financial planning and investing.

Up until now, I've had many family, friends, acquaintances and clients ask me for advice around financial planning and investing. And I have literally written an essay trying to give some advice around what I thought would be the best course of action for some. I still love giving advice, it's the one thing that honestly keeps me going and feels good when I'm able to help someone. But I'm also a firm believer of,

"Feed a man a fish and you feed him for a day. Teach a man to fish and you feed him for a lifetime."

Again, you don't need to know everything on your own. You just need basic knowledge. Just with anything, the more you know, the more you'll be able to make of the advice you're given.

We live in the information age where there's so much information thrown at us on a daily basis. It's very easy to get overwhelmed with everything that's going. Don't get me wrong, I think we live in a wonderful era because amazing innovations occur in such short spans of time. I can't even imagine what we'll have access to in the next few years, never mine the next decades. But the more I think about it all, the more my head spins. That's when I need to pull myself back, have a decent cup of coffee and realize that I can only do what I'm capable of doing and that's taking life in strides.

We can only do so much, live your life to its fullest everyday. You've heard it before, live everyday like it's your last day. Never take anything for granted. And as I've said time and time again, keep it simple. There's no need to overcomplicate anything, you can achieve what you need to achieve by keeping everything simple. Achieving financial freedom is no different. There is no right answer. Create a plan and stick to it, it'll all turn out alright in the end unless you create the most twisted plan ever, which I doubt you will if you read this book!

Stay positive and keep moving forward. Life is full of great opportunities, findings, and encounters. Be happy! Everything is possible if you give it a chance. Good luck!

Remember!

"Do or Do not. There is no try" – Master Yoda

www.ingramcontent.com/pod-product-compliance
Lightning Source LLC
Chambersburg PA
CBHW051334170526
45166CB00002B/814